Is it Possible to Communicate with the Dead?

The Loveday Method Part 3

A Journey You Will Never Forget.

The Third Book of a

Series of seven books.

*A Heptalogy:
By
Geoffrey Loveday*

Is it Possible to Communicate with the Dead?

Author: Geoffrey Loveday

Copyright © Geoffrey Loveday (2023)

The right of Geoffrey Loveday to be identified as author of this work has been asserted by the author in accordance with section 77 and 78 of the Copyright, Designs and Patents Act 1988.

First Published in 2023

ISBN 978-1-83538-006-2 (Hardback)
     978-1-83538-005-5 (Paperback)
     978-1-83538-028-4 (E-Book)

Published by:
    Maple Publishers
    Fairbourne Drive, Atterbury,
    Milton Keynes,
    MK10 9RG, UK
    www.maplepublishers.com

A CIP catalogue record for this title is available from the British Library.

All rights reserved. No part of this book may be reproduced or translated by any form or by any means, electronic or mechanical, including photocopying, recording or by any information storage and retrieval system without written permission from the author.

The views expressed in this work are solely those of the author and do not necessarily reflect the views of the publisher, and the publisher hereby disclaims any responsibility for them.

So come with me, and let me take you on a magical journey to see your loved ones, who have passed on, yet who will live on in your heart forever.

Gone but not forgotten.

I wonder where life will take us now...

And the journey begins.

Let me take you on this magical adventure.

Contents

Dedication: 7

Acknowledgement 9

Inspiration 11

Introduction 13

PART ONE 15

   A Magical Adventure of the Mind 16

   About the Author 21

   The Loveday Method 33

      The Magical Adventure of Life. 33

   Albert Einstein 36

      Einstein's theory about the mind 38

      The Infinite Power of Love 39

   Discovering New Truths 44

   The Magical Elixir of Hope 49

      Hope 51

The Greatest Mystery: The Meaning of Life? 56

A Spiritual Quest 62

   Unlocking the Mysteries of the Third Eye 63

   The Benefits of Opening the Third Eye 64

Meditation 66

Creating Life Before We Are Born 69

Déjà vu 72

PART TWO 75

Is it possible to communicate with the dead? 76

The Day of the Dead 79

Japan's Preserved Family Traditions 81

The loss of someone we love 86

The Celestial Connection: A Magical Voyage to Heal the Heart 89

PART THREE 93

A Magical Story of Belief. 94

Elaine's Story 96

Reliving The Past 102

Tony's Story 102

Dianne's Story 113

James' Story 117

Magical Journey with Sarah. 125

Amy's Story 135

Unknown's Story 139

Daniel's Story 144

The Sinking of the Lusitania. 152

Paul's Journey 161

Jan's Story 188

Sarah's Story 191

Leah's Story 199
PART FOUR 202
   All About You 203
   Visualisation and Meditation. 205
PART FIVE 209
   Belief 210
PART SIX 212
   The Journey 213
      Stage 1: The Pre-Talk 213
      Stage 2: Depth of Trance. 213
   Bibliography 216

Dedication:

My beautiful and courageous wife...

This book is not just a collection of words, but a testament to the love and strength of a woman who touched the hearts of those around her. My beautiful and courageous wife was taken from us at a far too early age, leaving behind a void that cannot be filled. Her children and I miss her every single day, and the ache in our hearts serves as a constant reminder of the incredible woman that we were blessed to have known and loved.

Despite the pain of our loss, my wife's spirit lives on as an enduring source of inspiration. She was a shining example of what it means to live life with courage, kindness, and grace. Her unwavering strength in the face of adversity, her selflessness, and her unconditional love touched the lives of all who knew her, and her memory will continue to inspire us in everything we do.

This book is dedicated to my wife, a woman whose legacy of love and bravery will forever be etched in our hearts. Though we may never fully heal from the pain of losing her, we take comfort in the knowledge that her light continues to shine on, guiding us through life's most difficult moments.

Acknowledgement

To my beautiful family...

I want to express my deepest gratitude for all the love and support you have shown me. You have been my rock, my guiding light, and my inspiration in times of joy and sorrow.

There were moments in my life when I felt lost and alone, when the weight of the world seemed too heavy to bear. But you never gave up on me. You were always there, standing by my side, holding my hand, and giving me the courage to face life's challenges.

Your unwavering belief in me, even when I didn't believe in myself, has been the driving force behind everything I've accomplished. Your love has given me the strength to push through the darkest moments and emerge stronger on the other side.

I am so grateful for every sacrifice you have made, every tear you have shed, and every prayer you have offered on my behalf. You are the beating heart of my life, and I am blessed to call you my family.

Thank you for never giving up on me, for always believing in me, and for being the loving and supportive family that I needed to thrive. I love you more than words can express.

Inspiration

To all the people who have lost their loved ones...

To anyone who has experienced the heart-wrenching pain of losing a loved one, I want you to know that you are not alone. The road ahead may seem insurmountable, but I urge you to have faith in your own strength and resilience. It takes an immense amount of courage to face each day when the world around you seems so bleak, and yet so many of us have found the inner fortitude to keep going.

The loss of a loved one can leave us feeling lost and helpless, but I urge you to take comfort in the memories you have shared. Though they may no longer be with us in body, their spirit lives on in the love and warmth that they brought to our lives. Every moment we shared with them was a precious gift, and their legacy will continue to inspire us for years to come.

In the face of such immense grief, it can be tempting to give up, to succumb to the weight of our pain. But I implore you, do not give up. Your loved one would not want you to live a life consumed by sadness and despair.

Instead, they would want you to live your life to the fullest, embracing each moment with the same joy and passion that they brought to your life.

So to all of you who have lost someone dear, I offer you my deepest condolences. But I also offer you my unwavering support and admiration for the courage you have shown in facing life's greatest challenges. May you find the strength to carry on, knowing that you are loved and never alone.

Introduction

Each story is different. We will examine their lives and together we will find the answers.

So I invite you, the reader, to join me on a journey to discover the causes of such widespread human misery found in the world today.

This is about their pain, and their suffering.

Inherited Therapy® and The Loveday Method® are one of my newest approaches in helping people overcome many of the problems and symptoms that are holding them back from living a happy and fulfilling life.

I am a full-time professional hypnotherapist and practitioner in pure–hypnoanalysis, as well as a Certified Hypnosis Instructor. And now, much to my surprise, the author of three books entitled:

Are You Reliving Someone Else's Life? The Loveday Method

The Invisible Force Affecting Our Children. The Loveday Method Part 2

Is it Possible to Communicate with the Dead? The Loveday Method Part 3, A Journey You Will Never Forget.

PART ONE

A lesson to be learned

A Magical Adventure of the Mind

"Once upon a time, there was a young woman named Ria who lived in a small village. She was known throughout the village for her beauty and her kind heart. She had a deep love for her parents, who had raised her from a young age.

"One day, tragedy struck. Her parents were killed in a terrible accident, leaving her all alone and heartbroken. She was inconsolable and found it hard to even get out of bed in the morning.

"Desperate to help their friend, the villagers went to the local wise woman, asking for her guidance. The wise woman was a renowned healer, known for her ability to unlock the mysteries of the mind and heal the body.

"She listened patiently to their concerns, and then invited the young woman into her home. There, she taught her the power of visualisation, and how to use it to unlock the mysteries of her mind.

"Close your eyes, Ria," she said. "Imagine yourself surrounded by a warm, healing light. Imagine your parents standing before you, smiling and healthy. Take their hands, and let them lead you on a journey."

"She did as she was told, and soon found herself transported to a beautiful garden. Her parents were beside her, holding her hands and guiding her on a walk through the garden.

"As they walked, Ria felt the warmth of the sun on her skin, the scent of flowers in the air, and the joy of being with her parents once again. She laughed and chatted with them, feeling her heart begin to heal.

"When the journey was over, she felt transformed. She was still grieving, but she had unlocked the mysteries of her mind and found a way to ease her pain.

"From that day on, Ria visited the wise woman regularly, always leaving feeling more at peace. And whenever she missed her parents, she would close her eyes and journey to the beautiful garden they had shown her, feeling their love and presence with her always.

"The villagers watched in awe as Ria slowly began to heal. They marvelled at the power of the wise *woman's teachings and the incredible healing power of the mind."*

❖

The mind is a fascinating and enigmatic realm, full of wonders and secrets waiting to be discovered. It is the place where our thoughts, emotions, memories, and beliefs reside, shaping who we are and how we experience the world around us. The human mind is a complex and intricate system, with countless neural pathways and connections that allow us to perceive, reason, and create.

As we delve deeper into the mysterious world of the mind, we will encounter a plethora of fascinating phenomena. We will discover the hidden workings of the subconscious, explore the depths of the unconscious, and unlock the secrets of the human psyche.

We will unravel the mysteries of mental illness and learn about the fascinating ways in which the brain can be rewired and transformed through neuroplasticity. Neuroplasticity is the brain's ability to reorganise itself by forming new neural connections throughout a person's life.

Through our journey, we will encounter a vast array of intriguing characters, from brilliant scientists to tortured artists, all of whom have made remarkable contributions to our understanding of the mind.

We will witness the incredible power of the human imagination and the ways in which it can shape our perception of reality.

So come with me on this thrilling adventure into the unknown depths of the mind. Together, we will explore the mysteries that lie within, and unlock the secrets of this most enigmatic and wondrous realm using The Loveday Method.

The Loveday Method is an advanced technique for travelling back in time through one's own consciousness in order to access dormant memories that are stored within one's DNA and are to blame for generational trauma.

The purpose of this treatment is to provide therapy for traumas that have been present in the family for a great many years and to uncover the mysteries that are hidden within our Genes and consciousness.

Discover This Mind-Blowing Formula...

Imagine if it were possible to use the power of your mind and The Loveday Method to open a doorway into your subconscious, where you could connect with the people you have lost and have meaningful conversations with them.

How incredible would it be to see their faces again, hear their voices, and feel their presence in a way that transcends time and space?

Where you could tap into the limitless potential of your subconscious mind and experience a profound sense of comfort, healing, and closure.

This is a truly remarkable possibility that holds immense promise for those who seek to connect with their loved ones who have passed on.

About the Author

The words you are about to read were inspired by a passage from my first book, and they provide insight into the suffering I experienced.

A little about me? I believe that it is only right to provide you with some insight into who I am. We all have a story to tell, and although I can't pretend to know how you're now feeling, I do know how it affected me.

I'd like to introduce myself. My name is Geoffrey Elliott Loveday, and I work as a hypnotherapist. I have worked with people who have struggled with PTSD, OCD, drug issues, depression, anxiety, and a variety of other disorders that are considered to be incapacitating for more than forty years. A good many of these individuals came to me lost in life.

My mother was diagnosed with breast cancer when I was 14 years old, and regrettably, she lost her battle with the disease not long afterwards. My life came crashing down when Mom passed away since she was the anchor of our family and such a wonderful source of motivation. Everything I ever learned and everything I ever owned was taken away from me. It is vital to understand that my mother served as the matriarch of our family and that my father lost a part of himself when my mom died.

I woke up one morning and I knew that my life would change forever, and nothing would be the same again. When my dad woke me up and told me my mum had died, it didn't really hit me at the time, and I don't think it ever did. Even to this day, maybe I'm still in a state of shock, or maybe it was a dream and soon I'll wake up from this nightmare.

It suddenly hit me I would never see my mum again, and as I am sitting here writing I have tears in my eyes. Even to this day, the pain never goes away, and we never forget. You see, I never got to know my mum, and that is so sad. I was a child lost and alone, and finding that life can be so unfair.

Unbeknownst to me, the universe had other plans for me, and life would take me on another path. Life is so unpredictable; it can change in a second.

Shortly after, I met Jackie, my lovely and fantastic wife. We dated for four years before marrying, and my only regret is that I should've married her the moment I saw her. We had five beautiful children after we married. Jackie was my soul mate and the love of my life.

However, my world was about to be devastated once again. Jackie was 39 years old when she was diagnosed with breast cancer. She died at home two years later. She was the most courageous and inspiring individual who ever walked the earth's surface. She contributed to a better world.

My world was falling around me once again. My prior life experiences, however, had given me the inner ability to deal with this. I couldn't and wouldn't give up; my children's world had crumbled, and all they had was me. I was never going to disappoint them.

I remember standing outside; unable to understand why the world was still moving. My world had just collapsed. How sad I felt. I wanted time to stand still, but life was not like that.

I looked around and I wanted everything to stop, but nothing did, and at that moment I realised everything moves forward in life.

I've been on a magnificent adventure throughout my life, and what a wonderful experience it has been. Life is a journey, and you can make it anything you choose.

Would I want to go back in time and make changes if I could? No, it has helped me get to where I am now. My experiences have given me the ability to properly listen to others, comprehend their suffering, and, most importantly, identify the cause of that suffering.

People who have benefited from my work with the power within have been able to identify the underlying causes of their persistent bodily and emotional ailments. Individuals have been able to face their ancestors, who carried on this pain, thanks to the work I've done to uncover the trauma. Those I have worked with have 'met' family members known and unknown.

Some are no longer with us. Secrets have been uncovered. And, recognising and treating this misery has relieved their suffering while also preventing future generations from suffering in the same way.

One of the most painful experiences of our lives is losing someone we love.

The death of a loved one is undoubtedly one of the most difficult experiences in life. Not only do we have to cope with our grief, but we also need to be there for others who are grieving as well. It can feel overwhelming and isolating at times, yet it's important to remember that you are not alone in your loss.

The people who love us can provide an invaluable source of support during this time. Whether it's a hug, a kind word, or a gesture of understanding, having someone who understands the sadness and longing you're feeling can be a great comfort. It can also give us a sense of connection to our loved ones and help us remember that their spirit lives on even in the absence of their physical presence.

We may not always know what to say or do when someone we love is grieving. But by simply listening to their stories and being there with them in their sorrow, we can be a comforting presence during this difficult time. We may not be able to take away the pain of loss, but we can offer our support and be a source of strength for those who are grieving.

It's simply just being there; even the smallest gestures can make all the difference in helping us cope with our grief. By recognising that we are connected and that we can rely on each other in times of sorrow, we can make the journey through grief a little bit easier.

No matter how difficult it may be to cope with the loss of someone you love, remember that your loved one lives on in your heart and memory. And by offering our support and understanding to those who are grieving, we can help each other heal.

No one should have to go through the loss of a loved one alone and by reaching out to those in need we can ensure that no one does. Together, we can help each other remember and honour the lives of our beloved ones even in their absence. Allowing ourselves to grieve together is not only a way to cope, but a way to keep the memory of our loved ones alive.

By coming together during times of grief and loss, we can provide comfort to one another and create lasting bonds that will help us through these difficult moments. So let us all make it a priority to be there for each other during times of sorrow and to honour the lives of those we have lost. Together, we can make it through any storm.

Together, we are stronger.

It's normal to isolate ourselves in times of sadness, but you can't afford to do so since others rely on you. How we handle grief has an enormous impact on the people we care about.

Can our past have a significant influence on our lives today? The answer to this question is an unequivocal, yes. Our past experiences, whether good or bad, can shape the way we view and interact with the world around us. They can set limits on our potential as well as open up new possibilities for growth and development.

When faced with difficult situations, people often draw upon their past experiences in order to make decisions and come up with solutions. We may also feel anchored to our past experiences by carrying unhealthy patterns of behaviour, such as self-doubt or negative thinking. Therefore, it is essential that we are mindful of the impact our history can have on our current lives in order to ensure that we are making healthy choices that will benefit us in the present.

Our past experiences can also be used to our advantage by helping us recognise and build upon our strengths. If we can take a step back and reflect on how far we have come, it can be motivating and inspire us to continue striving for success. By recognising the impact of our history, both positive and negative,

We can make more conscious decisions about our future and work towards living a life that is fulfilling and meaningful. In summary, it is safe to say that our past experiences do have a significant impact on our lives today. It is important to acknowledge the power of our history in order to create positive changes and take control of our lives.

Only then can we move forward and create a better future for ourselves. That said, it is also important to remember that how we respond to our past experiences will determine the direction of our lives today. We have the power to choose how we want our story to unfold and ultimately shape our present state.

By acknowledging and understanding the impact that our past experiences can have on our lives today, we can make more conscious decisions and strive to live a life full of purpose and meaning. We must learn to view our history as an opportunity to grow and be the best versions of ourselves.

Now is it possible our DNA affects our lives today? Yes, it is possible that our DNA can affect our lives today. Our genetic code contains information about our physical and mental traits, which can influence the way we react to different situations and experiences. These genetic predispositions may make us more or less susceptible to certain illnesses, behavioural tendencies, and even educational outcomes.

Therefore, it is important to understand our genetic makeup in order to make informed decisions about our healthcare, lifestyle choices, and overall well-being. Research is also ongoing into how environmental factors can interact with our DNA to shape the way we respond to different situations. For example, research suggests that childhood experiences can alter the expression of certain genes and even lead to epigenetic changes.

Are we holding onto the pain and suffering from our ancestors? We are still carrying the pain and suffering from our ancestors. Through intergenerational trauma, many of us have inherited certain traumas and emotional disturbances, which can manifest in various ways throughout our lives. These may include difficulties in forming relationships, trust issues and behavioural problems. Research has also shown that a traumatic experience can be passed down through generations in the form of epigenetic changes.

This means that even if we have not directly experienced a traumatic event ourselves, we may still carry its impacts in our DNA. It is important to recognise this and work towards healing any lingering pain or trauma from our ancestors. Doing so can help us move forward with greater clarity and understanding, allowing us to create a better future for ourselves and our descendants. In conclusion, it is clear that our past experiences can have a significant impact on our lives today.

It is possible that our DNA may be affected by both genetic and environmental factors, while we may also be holding onto the pain and suffering of our ancestors. By understanding and acknowledging the power of our history, we can work towards making proactive choices and striving for a future that is full of purpose and meaning. Only then can we move forward and create a better life for ourselves.

Only then can we move forward and live a life that is full of purpose and meaning. With the right knowledge and understanding, we can make proactive choices that will help us live a life we are truly proud of.

Ultimately, our past can be a powerful tool that we can use to create a better life for ourselves and those around us.

Just suppose there was a method to reverse the effects of the pain and suffering that we are currently experiencing by travelling back in time?

A way let go of the traumas we are holding onto and return them back to our ancestors.

Search no further...

The Loveday Method

The Loveday Method is a cutting-edge method for accessing dormant memories that are held in one's Genetics and are to blame for genetic pain. It involves travelling back in time through one's own subconscious.

The objective of this treatment is to unearth the secrets that are buried in our genes and mind as well as to provide therapy for traumas that have been present in the family from before we were born...

The Magical Adventure of Life.

Life is indeed a magical adventure, full of twists and turns, highs and lows, and unexpected surprises. It is a journey that begins the moment we are born, and continues until the moment we take our last breath.

As we venture forth on this adventure, we encounter a myriad of experiences that shape us and help us grow. We learn to crawl before we walk, and stumble before we run. We make friends, fall in love, and experience heartbreak. We discover our passions, face our fears, and overcome challenges.

Along the way, we also encounter moments of pure magic. We witness the beauty of a sunset, the majesty of a mountain range, or the wonder of a star-filled sky. We experience the joy of laughter, the warmth of a hug, or the thrill of a first kiss. We create memories that will stay with us for a lifetime.

As we move through life, we are constantly evolving, learning, and growing. We may encounter obstacles or setbacks, but we also have the power to overcome them. We have the ability to shape our own destiny and to make our dreams a reality.

Ultimately, the magical adventure of life is about finding our purpose, discovering our passions, and living each day to the fullest. It is about embracing the journey, and enjoying every moment along the way. So let us treasure the magic of life, and cherish each and every experience that comes our way.

Every day, the magic of life is all around us. Life is a precious thing, yet so often we take it for granted. We forget to appreciate the small moments that make life special. The sun rising each morning or the laughter of children playing in the park; these are aspects of life that often go unnoticed. We don't have to look far for this everyday magic; it's all around us if we just open our eyes and hearts.

Taking a few moments each day to be mindful and take notice of the wondrous things in life can make a huge difference in our outlook on life. Life really is filled with magical moments; we just have to take the time to notice them. So open your eyes and hearts to the everyday magic of life; it's a truly amazing thing!

Albert Einstein

A man who made remarkable contributions to our understanding of the human experience, Albert Einstein's theories about the mind are often referred to as "The Theory of Relativity" and can be found in his famous book, The Relativity: The Special and General Theory.

In this work, Einstein developed a thought-provoking view of how space and time interact with each other and how physical objects change depending on their relative motion.

He also proposed the idea of "relativity of simultaneity," which suggests that time passes differently for different observers depending on their relative speed and position.

These ideas have become integral to modern physics, allowing scientists to understand phenomena such as gravity, black holes, and even the structure of the universe itself.

In addition to his work in physics, Einstein is also credited with making significant contributions to the understanding of human thought and behaviour, including his famous quote: "Imagination is more important than knowledge", which reflects his belief that creative problem-solving and abstract thought should be valued over rote memorisation.

In his later years, Einstein wrote extensively on philosophy, noting that the only way to truly understand the world is through experience and intuition.

He argued that while scientific knowledge can help us understand how the universe works, it cannot explain why it exists or what purpose it serves; questions that can only be answered through deeper contemplation.

By combining empirical evidence with a thoughtful examination of life, Einstein hoped to gain insight into the mysteries of the universe and humanity's place within it.

In summary, Albert Einstein's theories about the mind encompass a wide range of topics including space-time, physical objects, relativity of simultaneity, and creativity can lead to greater insight and understanding. Ultimately, Einstein's theories about the mind show us how we should look at problems from multiple perspectives in order to gain deeper insight and knowledge.

"Imagination is more important than knowledge,"
Albert Einstein[1]

Einstein's theory about the mind

Albert Einstein famously said that "the mind that is opened to new ideas never comes back to its original size." He believed that the human mind was capable of forming new connections and understanding concepts far beyond our initial potential.

This idea has been echoed by modern scientists, who recognise the power of the brain to continuously develop and grow. Einstein's theory of the mind has been used to explain the process of learning, creativity, and problem solving. It is also used to understand how knowledge is stored in the brain, and how our mental abilities can be improved with practice.

---

[1] https://en.wikipedia.org/wiki/Albert_Einstein

In short, Einstein's theory of the mind emphasises the importance of cultivating an open mindset that encourages intellectual growth. This theory has been widely adopted by educational institutions, businesses, and individuals as a way to further their own understanding and success. Through this theory, we can gain insight into how the brain works and learn to unlock its full potential.

By continuing to challenge ourselves intellectually, we can constantly be pushing our mental boundaries in order to reach new heights of understanding. This is something that Einstein believed in deeply and his theory of the mind is still relevant today.

Through further study, we can learn more about how our minds work and how to better use them in order to expand our knowledge. By doing so, we can make great strides in realising our potential for success and growth. Albert Einstein's theory of the mind is a timeless reminder that our minds have limitless potential, and that we should strive to unlock it.

The Infinite Power of Love

A Letter from Albert Einstein to His Daughter[2]

Albert Einstein's letter to his daughter on the universal force of love was a beautiful expression of his belief in the power of love as the fundamental force that governs the universe.

This power combines everything and gives life its purpose.

In the letter, Einstein emphasised that love is not merely an emotion between individuals, but rather a universal force that binds everything together. He explained that love is a force that transcends time and space, and that it is the ultimate power that drives the cosmos.

Einstein also wrote about the importance of cultivating empathy and compassion for others, and how these qualities are essential for leading a fulfilling life. He believed that love and compassion were essential for creating a peaceful and harmonious world.

---

[2] https://community.thriveglobal.com/einstein-letter-to-his-daughter-on-the-universal-force-of-love/

Overall, Einstein's letter to his daughter conveyed a profound message about the significance of love as a force that unites all things and the importance of cultivating love and compassion in our lives.

In this passage of the letter he wrote to his daughter, Albert Einstein highlights the failure of humanity in the use and control of other forces of the universe, which have turned against us.

He believes that it is urgent that we nourish ourselves with another kind of energy if we want our species to survive, find meaning in life, and save the world, and every sentient being that inhabits it. According to Einstein, this energy is love.

Einstein's message is a powerful one. He suggests that our current way of using and controlling the forces of the universe has not been sustainable, and this has resulted in significant consequences for our planet and its inhabitants.

He seems to be referring to the many ways in which humanity has exploited the natural world, from pollution and deforestation to the depletion of natural resources.

But what is this other kind of energy that we need to nourish ourselves? Einstein believes that it is love. He argues that if we want to save our species and the world, we need to embrace a new way of being, one that is centred on love rather than power and control.

Love, in this sense, is not simply a feeling of affection or attachment. Instead, it is a way of relating to the world that involves compassion, empathy, and a deep sense of connection to all living beings. When we act out of love, we are motivated not by self-interest or a desire for power, but by a genuine concern for the well-being of others.

Einstein's message is a call to action. He is urging us to reject the old ways of doing things and embrace a new way of being. This means treating the natural world and all its inhabitants with care and respect, rather than exploiting them for our own ends. It also means cultivating a sense of compassion and empathy for all living beings, human and non-human alike.

In conclusion, Einstein's message is a powerful one that speaks to the urgent need for humanity to change its ways. By embracing love as the one and only answer to our problems, we can create a better world for ourselves and all living beings.

Discovering New Truths

The world is no longer a mysterious place; there are no more places or continents to discover; even the most remote places in deepest, darkest Africa are now mapped out.

People still seek out the unknown because they believe that is what advances humanity.

Isn't it about time that we began to investigate the unfathomable workings of the mind?

How do we continue to explore our minds to discover new truths, or even just a better understanding of who we are? This is the realm of psychology and neuroscience. Through research in these areas, people are looking at ways to understand how the brain works and exploring the various effects different psychological states can have on us.

Through this research, scientists hope to gain a better understanding of how to treat mental illnesses, as well as optimise our wellbeing in everyday life. For example, research has shown that regular physical activity can help improve mood and reduce stress levels.

Additionally, we now know that mindfulness-based practices can help us to better manage difficult emotions and develop greater emotional resilience. Ultimately, new knowledge and understanding of the mind can help us all to live better, more fulfilling lives.

In order for us to continue to explore and understand our minds, we need access to reliable information about psychology and neuroscience. Academic journals are a great source of knowledge, but they also tend to be difficult to interpret and comprehend.

That's why many organisations have emerged to provide educational resources and courses that are designed to teach people about the science of the mind. These organisations can provide us with a more accessible way of learning, allowing us to better understand how our minds work and, in turn, develop better ways of living.

With this knowledge at hand, we can then look at practical applications. For example, we can use what we know about the brain and psychology to develop better mental health treatments, or create technology that is better adapted to our needs.

We can also use this understanding of the mind to improve our relationships with others, as well as build stronger communities.

Ultimately, psychological research has revolutionised how we look at the world and understand ourselves. By continuing to explore and learn more about the science of the mind, we can continuously improve our lives.

So let's keep on exploring and discover what lies hidden in the depths of our minds!

But let's say for a moment that there was another way to study the mind, using The Loveday Method.

The Loveday Method is a sophisticated method of mentally retracing one's ancestors' steps in order to retrieve the repressed memories that have been passed down through the generations and are responsible for suffering affecting the world today.

The purpose of this treatment is to help families work through long-standing memories and to discover the secrets buried within our DNA and our minds.

Imagine for a minute the discoveries we could make and the adventure we could take. And the ways in which it would reduce the suffering that exists in the world today.

How do we take the sadness away after losing someone we love? There is no easy answer to this difficult question. Each person's experience of grief and mourning is unique, so there isn't a one-size-fits-all solution. However, there are some things that can help us move through the pain of grief and begin to heal.

First and foremost, it's important to give yourself permission to feel what you're feeling. Grief is a natural reaction to the loss of someone we love and it can manifest in many different ways; including sadness, anger, guilt, and confusion. Allowing yourself to experience your emotions instead of trying to suppress them can help you move through the grieving process at a healthier pace.

Talking about your loss with supportive friends and family can also help. Sharing memories of the person you lost, expressing your feelings, and finding comfort in the love of those who care about you can be extremely beneficial. Having a strong support system is an invaluable resource when it comes to healing from grief.

It's also important to give yourself time and space to grieve. Everyone experiences grief differently and it can take weeks, months, or even years to come to terms with the loss of a loved one. Allowing yourself time to heal and engaging in activities that bring you joy can help you cope with your grief.

Finally, if you feel overwhelmed by your emotions, seeking professional help is an option. Grief counsellors and therapists can provide a safe space to talk about your struggles and offer strategies for coping with the pain of loss.

Grieving is a difficult process, but it's important to remember that you are not alone. Finding love and support from those around you, allowing yourself time to heal, and taking advantage of professional help

Every story has a different meaning, but the story of self-belief is always the same...

The Magical Elixir of Hope

"Once upon a time, in a far-off land, there was a young girl named Celeste. Celeste had always suffered from a peculiar condition called OCD, which caused her to have unwanted, intrusive thoughts and compulsive behaviours that interfered with her daily life.

"As Celeste grew older, her condition worsened, and she felt increasingly isolated and alone. She longed for a solution that would not only help her but also the countless others who suffered from similar conditions all over the world.

"One day, while wandering through a magical forest, Celeste stumbled upon a mystical clearing. In the centre of the clearing, she saw a shimmering pool of water, and beside it stood a majestic unicorn.

"The unicorn sensed Celeste's distress and asked her what was troubling her. Celeste poured out her heart, telling the unicorn about her struggles with OCD and her desire to find a solution to help not only herself but also others who suffered.

"The unicorn listened patiently and then offered Celeste a magical elixir that would help her overcome her condition. But the unicorn also warned her that the elixir was very powerful and must be used with great care.

"Celeste drank the elixir and felt a sudden surge of energy coursing through her body. She felt her OCD symptoms starting to fade away, and a sense of calm and peace washed over her.

"Over the coming weeks and months, Celeste continued to use the elixir, carefully following the unicorn's instructions, and slowly but surely, her OCD symptoms disappeared entirely.

"Celeste was overjoyed and grateful to the unicorn for helping her overcome her condition. She knew that she could not keep this magical elixir to herself, and so she travelled far and wide, sharing the elixir with others who suffered from OCD and other similar conditions.

"As she journeyed, she discovered that the elixir not only helped people overcome their conditions but also gave them a newfound sense of hope and optimism for the future.

"In time, Celeste became known as the "Elixir of Light," and her story inspired countless others to never give up hope and to keep searching for solutions to their struggles, no matter how difficult they may seem.

"And so, Celeste's legacy lived on, as the magic of her elixir continued to transform lives and bring light to all who drank from its healing waters."

Hope

"To walk a thousand miles you need only put one foot in front of the other."

When hope is taken away, it can feel like a weight so heavy that you can't get up. Life may seem bleak and the future unsure of what will come next. It's easy to lose motivation when feeling like this.

But if there's one thing anyone can do in such circumstances, it's to take small but meaningful steps toward positivity. Reaching out for support and *engaging in meaningful activities can help you to stay motivated and get through hard times.*

Talk to a friend or family member, look into taking up a hobby, try different forms of self-care - these are all ways to begin the journey towards restoring hope within one's life.

Focusing on oneself and focusing on the good can help to break down feelings of hopelessness and to see a brighter future. It is never too late to start anew, pick yourself up and move forward with hope in your heart. No matter the situation, there will always be another opportunity for growth and happiness.

With determination, resilience and faith anything is possible. Don't give up; keep going. You are strong enough to overcome this difficulty and fill your life with hope once again.

No one should have to go through the pain of feeling hopeless on their own. If you or someone you know is struggling, seek out professional help and support services to work towards restoring hope. Even if it feels *like a mountain to climb, every step taken is a step closer to feeling better and gaining clarity.*

With the right resources, life can be faced with strength and hope. It takes courage to start again but it can lead you to a brighter future; don't ever give up!

Have faith that there will always be another opportunity for growth and happiness. Believe in yourself and that you can find hope again.

Take heart, you are not alone and there is always hope. Don't be discouraged, your future still awaits you. Reach out for help, surround yourself with support and positivity, and keep going; the world needs more of your light in it! Together we can find ways to restore hope in our lives and the lives of others.

Discovering peacefulness within when sadness overwhelms us is a difficult state to attain. Everyone experiences different levels of sadness and has different ways of finding solace.

That said, there are some universal steps that can be taken to help us find inner peace when we feel overwhelmed by our emotions:

1. *Take time for yourself: Make space in your day for moments where you can just be with yourself. Whether it is through meditation, yoga, or even just taking a walk in nature, set aside some time to be alone and take care of your emotional needs.*

2. *Connect with others: Talk to someone who you trust and who can open up about how you are feeling. Having people around us that understand our struggles and can lend a listening ear is often invaluable in getting through difficult times.*

3. *Find joy in the little things: It is easy to get bogged down by negative thoughts and emotions, so make sure you take time to appreciate the small moments of happiness that come your way each day. Whether it be a smile from a stranger, a beautiful sunset, or a good cup of coffee, take a moment to enjoy these moments and use them as a reminder that there is still joy in the world.*

4. *Practise self-compassion:* Sometimes being too hard on ourselves can add an extra layer of stress and difficulty. Learn to be kind to yourself and forgive yourself for not being perfect.

5. *Seek professional help:* If you find that your sadness is overwhelming and difficult to manage, don't be afraid to seek out medical help or counselling. A professional can provide invaluable insight and support in times of distress.

By following these steps, we can take small but essential steps towards finding inner peace when sadness overwhelms us. It is important to remember that the journey towards emotional well-being is a process and takes time, so be gentle with yourself as you take these steps forward.

The Greatest Mystery: The Meaning of Life?

This is one of the most challenging questions to answer, as it can vary greatly depending on individual beliefs and values.

Ultimately, the meaning of life lies in the eye of the beholder. For some people, living a meaningful life may involve pursuing their passions, striving for excellence, and making a positive impact on society.

For others, it could mean spending quality time with family and friends, helping those in need, or finding peace within oneself. There is no single answer to this question, as each person's interpretation of it will be unique.

What matters most is that one finds meaning in life by whatever they deem appropriate and fulfilling. Ultimately, the key is to live according to your values and finding contentment. By doing so, you will be able to find fulfilment, joy, and satisfaction in life regardless of the circumstances.

In this way, you can create a life that is truly meaningful for yourself. At the end of the day, what matters most is that you find meaning in the life that you are living.

Life is a journey and it is up to you to make the most of it. By living your life in accordance with your values, you can create true happiness for yourself. Finding the meaning of life is an ongoing process that we must all go through in order to find our own personal purpose and fulfilment.

The key is to keep an open mind and embrace life's journey as it comes. By taking the time to consider what matters most to you and living according to your values, you can find true meaning. Remember it is up to you.

Find your own personal purpose and create a meaningful life for yourself! Once you do, you will be able to find true joy.

The question we need to ask ourselves is: "What is life and why are we here?"

This can be seen differently depending on a person's individual perspective. Some believe that life is a process of self-discovery, growth, and development—a journey of learning in which our experiences shape us into who we ultimately become.

Others view life as an opportunity for humans to fulfil their purpose or leave a lasting legacy. Ultimately, life is an experience that each one of us has the agency to define in our own unique way.

No matter what you believe, it is clear that life can be filled with joy and sorrow, successes and failures; and that all of these experiences serve to make us stronger as individuals when we take time to reflect and appreciate them. We are here to make the most of life, whatever that may mean to each of us.

Life is a journey, not a destination. It is important to remember that we should focus on the present and strive for the future, while still finding joy in each day and taking time to appreciate our experiences along the way.

We should strive to make the most of our time here, living with purpose and intent, and finding fulfilment in whatever it is that fulfils us. Life is too short to waste; it is up to each of us to create the life we want!

No matter where we are in our lives or what lies ahead, it is important to remember that we are here for a reason. None of us can ever know the answer to why we are here, but what matters is that each one of us makes the most out of our lives and finds fulfilment in whatever it may be; because truly, life is what we make it.

Why is it that we have such advanced technology, yet our understanding of the potential of the human intellect is so limited?

Despite technological advancements, the majority of us are only just beginning to understand our mental capacities. We now know that our brains can do much more than we previously thought.

Through neuroscience, artificial intelligence, and the radical transformation of learning models, humans are being granted access to capabilities that were once unimaginable.

The human mind is capable of extraordinary feats – from extraordinary acts of creativity and problem-solving to the capacity for abstract thought and complex emotions.

Yet, despite this power, our understanding of how to best tap into it is still in its infancy. A key challenge lies in the fact that traditional education models are still not designed to leverage our full potential.

The education system needs to be adapted to ensure that people are provided with the opportunity for self-expression and personal growth; not just in terms of knowledge but also in terms of emotional, social, and cognitive development.

Moreover, recent advances in technology have made it easier to access data and develop new solutions to challenges faced by our generation.

For example, artificial intelligence (AI) has enabled us to develop powerful solutions for problems such as healthcare, transportation, and energy. AI can also enable people to think more deeply about their lives - from financial decisions to career paths, without having to rely solely on intuition or fortune-telling. In this way, technology can open up new possibilities that were once beyond reach.

The potential of the human mind is immense and, with the right combination of technology and education, we can unlock its full capacity. With the right tools, we can create a world where everyone has access to opportunities that unlock their unique talents and dreams.

We have a long way to go before we understand how best to tap into our collective intellect, but the journey has already begun.

By understanding our own potential, and leveraging advances in technology to help us reach it, we can create a more equitable and prosperous future for everyone.

A Spiritual Quest

Let's step outside of the world of medicine for a moment to begin searching for solutions. What we are capable of and what is our true potential?

Let us dive deep into that mysterious question; what exactly is The Third Eye?

The third eye, a spiritual concept located between the physical eyes on the forehead, offers perception beyond the ordinary. Believed to connect with the Pineal Gland regulating sleep and rhythms, opening it enhances intuition, clairvoyance, and spiritual connection.

Opening the third eye is achieved through practices like meditation, yoga, breathing exercises, and visualization. Patience and dedication are key as it's an ongoing journey of self-discovery.

Benefits include heightened intuition, creativity, and a deeper understanding of spirituality. Opening it may lead to a sense of oneness, improved decision-making, and vivid experiences.

Signs of an open third eye include tingling between the eyebrows, heightened intuition, vivid dreams, enhanced colour perception, and improved clarity of thought. While results may not be immediate, perseverance and practice can help unlock its potential.

Unlocking the Mysteries of the Third Eye

Opening the third eye can be done in a variety of ways, including meditation, yoga, breathing work, and visualisation.

1. *1. Meditation is an excellent practice, as it allows us to tap into deeper states of awareness and connect with our spiritual selves.*

2. *Deep breathing exercises such as pranayama can help also, as they stimulate the pineal gland and help to increase our awareness.*

3. *Visualisation techniques can also be used, by focusing on a mental image of a bright light or energy in between your physical eyes.*

4. *Practising yoga can also help, as certain poses can help to improve circulation in the body and create a sense of calm and balance.*

All of these techniques can help to open the third eye, but it is important to be patient and take your time.

The Benefits of Opening the Third Eye

Opening the third eye can bring many benefits, such as an enhanced sense of intuition and insight into the world around you.

They may notice an increase in creativity and mental clarity, as well as a deeper understanding of the spiritual world.

Also report feeling a sense of oneness and connectedness to all things, as well as an increased ability to manifest their desires and access deeper forms of knowledge.

Additionally, they often report greater clarity when making decisions or forming opinions about important matters.

Ultimately it is a powerful journey of self-discovery and spiritual growth that can bring great rewards.[3]

---
[3] https://en.wikipedia.org/wiki/Third_eye

Meditation

How should one go about quieting the mind? Is meditation effective? What kind of meditation works the best?

The best way to meditate is to find a comfortable, quiet place where you will be undisturbed. It can be indoors or outdoors; it's up to you. Take a few deep breaths and relax your body. Focus on your breathing, the rhythm of the air entering and leaving your body, or even count each breath if it helps you stay focused.

Allow any thoughts that arise to naturally come and go without judgement. If your mind starts to wander, simply bring it back to the focus of your meditation.

The goal is not to clear your mind but rather to become aware of your thoughts without getting attached to or distracted by them.

You can meditate for as little as five minutes a day or longer if you wish. Make sure to practise regularly, as it can have many positive benefits.

With consistent meditation, you will slowly experience more clarity, peace, and insight into yourself.

Meditation doesn't require any special equipment or props; all you need is your breath and a space where you can sit comfortably.

That being said, some people prefer to use tools such as cushions, blankets, or benches to help support their posture while they meditate. It's entirely up to you and what works best for your body and mind.

If you're just starting out with meditation, it's recommended that you start small—a few minutes a day—and gradually increase the time as you become more comfortable with the practice.

Finally, remember that meditation can take many forms—you don't have to stick to just one way of meditating. Experiment and see what works for you!

A good rule of thumb is that any practice which calms and quiets your mind will be beneficial. Start with just one or two techniques, and then add on more as you become more experienced in meditating.

Above all, remain consistent; meditation works best when practised regularly.

Meditating can help reduce stress and anxiety, improve focus and concentration, and foster inner peace and clarity, and much more.

So give it a try—you just might be surprised at the results! With patience, dedication, and practice you will soon find yourself in a calmer state of mind. Enjoy your meditation journey!

"We cannot change the past but we can learn from it."
Geoffrey E. Loveday

Creating Life Before We Are Born

Is it possible that we created our life before we were born?

The idea that we can create our life before we are born is an intriguing concept that has been explored by spiritualists and metaphysicians alike. On the surface, this notion may appear to be far-fetched; however, there is evidence to suggest that it could be true.

One line of thinking related to this idea comes from the field of quantum mechanics. This branch of science suggests that we all exist in a vast, interconnected reality where we can influence and shape our destiny through the power of thought and intention.

This means that we could be subconsciously creating our own lives before being born into physical form.

Another concept related to this idea comes from near-death experiences. People who have gone through this experience often report having memories of their past lives or a deep awareness that their current life was chosen consciously by them before birth.

Ultimately, the notion that we can create our life before we are born still remains largely speculative; however, it is an interesting concept to explore and has been the source of much fascination and debate.

While it may not be possible to definitively prove that we have the power to shape our destinies before birth, it is certainly worth considering and pondering over.

Whatever conclusion one draws from this notion, one thing remains certain: We are all capable of creating positive change in our lives by using the power of our intention and thought.

By applying this knowledge to our everyday lives, we can better understand how we are in control of our destinies.

I firmly believe that each person's story began long before they were born. We are not in control of our life, we are guided by an invisible force and unseen influence.

Your life is a map we never go in a straight line we are guided on a path we are supposed to take. We only have free will up to a point.

We cannot change the past, but we can learn from it. Everything that has ever happened is supposed to happen. If just one thing was out of place, you wouldn't have what you have now.

Take a few moments and read that sentence again.

If you could go back in time what would you change? Think for a moment before you answer that question.
Be careful what you wish for, by changing things you will lose what you already have.

All the sadness and happiness that we have are nature's way of strengthening us.

I firmly believe that I have visited this place numerous times in the past. My inner self tells me that I am an ancient who has lived here since the beginning of time, but I don't know if this is all in my imagination.

My intuition tells me that even though our family – parents, siblings, and children – are always with us, they may appear in various roles when we return.

The next time, I might be the father, my mother might be my sister, and my brother might be my child.

What I do know is that we are here for a reason and that the universe we live in is a classroom of learning.

You created your life before you were born. So what does that mean?

My feelings tell me that before we came to this planet we all sit around a table with our social group, all the people that we will meet and discuss the life that we will have then we do it for real.

There I was, ready to come to this world. I remember saying to myself I will remember everything. You know, when I arrived I couldn't remember a single thing. Would you believe, that is so annoying?

Dĕja vu

Have you ever had déjà vu?

Déjà vu is a phenomenon that occurs when people have the feeling of familiarity associated with a place, situation or event, even though they may never have experienced it before.

The feeling comes and goes quickly, leaving the person wondering why they felt so familiar with something they had never seen before. Scientists are still trying to understand why this phenomenon happens and what it could indicate.

One possible explanation is that the feeling of familiarity comes from a memory glitch in the brain, where a person mistakenly recalls an experience they had before, even though they haven't actually experienced it yet.

Another explanation is that people feel familiar with something because of their subconscious knowledge or intuition about the situation. This could be because of something they've heard from someone else, or information their minds have picked up from other sources like the media.

Whatever the cause may be, déjà vu is an interesting and mysterious occurrence that has puzzled scientists and laypeople alike for centuries.

No matter what the cause may be, it is clear that déjà vu is an intriguing experience and can offer insight into how our minds process memories and information.

In some cases, this phenomenon may even signal a change in our lives or indicate something important we need to pay attention to. Regardless of why people experience déjà vu, it will likely continue to be a fascinating phenomenon for years to come.

It is possible instances of déjà vu are triggered by the memories that can be traced all the way back to events that occurred centuries or even millions of years before our birth, as recorded in our DNA.

And that we are reliving someone else's life.

I suppose you are wondering what the title means and what the book is all about? Read on to find the answers.

PART TWO

Is it possible to communicate with the dead?

Is it possible to communicate with the dead?

Many believe that it is possible to communicate with those who have passed on. Through different mediums, people may attempt to connect with the spirits of those who are no longer living.

Some claim to be able to use a form of extrasensory perception (ESP) or telepathy, while others believe they can summon the spirits through Ouija boards or séances.

Regardless of how it is attempted, some believe that the dead can speak to us and give us messages from beyond this world.

Some might be sceptical of attempting to contact those who have passed, but there may still be a feeling of comfort in knowing that they are not gone forever.

Many cultures around the world have traditions that honour and remember the dead, such as Day of the Dead celebrations in Mexico or ancestor worship in Japan. Many different spiritual practices can be used to connect with those who have passed, such as prayer, meditation, ritual offerings, and more.

Ultimately, whether one believes it is possible to talk to the spirits of the dead or not, it is important to remember that those who have left this world are still with us in spirit. Through various forms of communication and remembrance, we can keep their memory alive and find comfort in feeling connected to them even after they are gone.

Cultures around the world offer a variety of ways to remember and honour the dead, from spiritual rituals to ceremonies. No matter how one chooses to remember their loved ones who have passed on, it is important to keep in mind that those we have lost are still with us in spirit and can still be a part of our lives.

The act of connecting with the deceased remains a highly personal choice. Each individual has their own way of honouring the spirits of those who have passed on, whether it be through rituals or remembrance ceremonies. With an open heart and a willingness to listen and learn, we can all find ways to connect with those who have gone before us in spirit.

For those who choose to reach out and try to connect with the spirits of those who have passed on, there are a few things to keep in mind. It is important to be respectful and open-minded, as well as patient when connecting with the dead. Though we may not always get an answer right away, or at all, it is important to remember that the spirits of those who have passed on are still with us and may be willing to communicate when we reach out.

Finding comfort in talking to and hearing from the dead can be a powerful tool in our lives, but it must not be taken lightly. It is important to respect boundaries and traditions when attempting contact and to only do so with an open and honest attitude. With love, patience, and respect, we can find peace in being able to connect with our loved ones who are no longer here in physical form.

At the end of the day, it is up to each individual to decide if they want to attempt to contact those who have passed on. Whether through spiritual rituals, séances, or other forms of communication, it is possible to connect with the spirits of those who have gone before us. With an open heart and mind, we can keep the memories of our loved ones alive and remain connected even after they are no longer here in physical form.

No matter how one chooses to remember and honour the dead, it is important to hold them close in spirit. Through various forms of communication, we can stay connected and keep their memory alive in our hearts forever.

The Day of the Dead

The Day of the Dead (Día de Los Muertos) is a traditional Mexican holiday that celebrates and honours those who have passed away. It is celebrated on November 1 and 2, with the main festivities taking place on the first day.

The holiday combines pre-Hispanic indigenous spiritual beliefs with traditions brought by Spanish conquistadors and Catholic missionaries, resulting in a vibrant and colourful celebration.

On the Day of the Dead, families visit cemeteries to decorate gravesites with flowers and offer food, drinks, and other offerings to their deceased loved ones as a symbol of respect.

Altars are also made at homes to remember those who have died, often with photographs, candles, and traditional food such as pan de Muerto (bread of the dead).

Celebrations are often accompanied by live music and other festivities. Whether it is through spiritual rituals or remembrance ceremonies, the Day of the Dead is a time to honour those who have passed away and celebrate their lives.

At the end of the day, it is ultimately up to each individual to find their own way of connecting with those who have passed on. With love and respect, we can keep our loved ones close in spirit, no matter how far away they may be.

No matter how we choose to remember and honour the dead, it is important to hold them close in spirit. Through spiritual practices, ceremonies, and other forms of communication, we can stay connected with those who are no longer here in physical form.

With an open heart and mind, we can keep the memories of our loved ones alive forever.

Japan's Preserved Family Traditions

In Japan, ancestor worship is an important part of the culture and history. It has been practised for thousands of years and is rooted in the belief that the spirits of deceased ancestors can influence the lives of their living descendants.

Ancestor worship involves a variety of rituals and ceremonies performed in honour of one's ancestors, including offerings to them such as food, drink, and flowers.

Offerings may also be made for special occasions such as weddings or funerals. The purpose of ancestor worship is to show respect and gratitude to one's ancestors, who are believed to bestow blessings upon their descendants in return.

It can also serve as a way of connecting with the past and preserving family traditions. In modern Japan, ancestor worship is still practised and remains an important part of the culture.

As such, it provides a link between generations and upholds the traditions of Japan's past while providing a sense of continuity in families across time.

While ancestor worship in Japan may not be as prevalent now as it once was, it is still an important part of the culture and has been passed down through generations.

It is a practice that honours those who came before us, while also providing comfort to those who remain. By acknowledging our ancestors, we can recognise the importance of family, faith, and tradition in our lives.

The rituals associated with ancestor worship serve as a reminder to appreciate what we have and honour the legacy of those before us.

The practice of ancestor worship in Japan is steeped in tradition and history, providing an important connection between past and present. It serves as a reminder that our ancestors are with us in spirit, offering guidance and protection.

With each generation, their influence lives on, reminding us to appreciate our family and pass down the values of the past to future generations. Through ancestor worship, we are able to honour those who came before us and ensure that their legacy lives on.

Ultimately, ancestor worship in Japan embodies a sense of respect and reverence for one's ancestors while connecting with the past.

It is an important part of Japan's history and culture, providing a meaningful way for families to remember their ancestors and carry on their legacy.

In Japan, ancestor worship is still practised today and provides an important link between generations. By honouring our ancestors in this way, we can ensure that the traditions of the past are preserved and remain part of our present lives.

Transformative Encounters with Mortality

A brush with death often leads to transformative shifts in people's perspectives and life choices.

Life-Altering Moments at Death's Door...

A near-death experience (NDE) is a mysterious event reported by those who feel they've come close to dying. These experiences often include sensations of peace, out-of-body observations, and even encounters with ethereal lights or beings.

People who have had NDEs frequently describe lasting changes in their life perspectives and overall outlook, generally tilting towards the positive.

While scientific and philosophical communities continue to explore the causes and implications of NDEs, no conclusive explanation exists. Nonetheless, the experiences often result in transformative personal impacts.

Debate and research persist, but what's clear is that NDEs have a significant, often life-altering effect on those who experience them. These extraordinary events remain a point of fascination and discussion, affecting each individual in a deeply personal way.

You Are Not Alone

Close your eyes and feel their presence, *the ones you've lost, watching over you, guiding you silently. Though physically absent, their love remains steadfast, nestled in your heart.*

To honour their memory, keep traditions alive, share their stories, and cherish their belongings. Love knows no bounds, even in death.

Grief is a tough journey, but those we've lost stay with us when we keep them alive in our hearts. Love endures; they are never truly gone.

Remember, love cannot be extinguished by death. You are loved and never forgotten. They are your guardians from above, always a part of you.

Hold their memories close; they are the essence of eternal love. Life is precious; love is forever. They live on in your heart.

Find peace and comfort in this knowledge during difficult times.

Now, imagine for a moment that there was another way...

The loss of someone we love

Have you lost someone?

Losing someone we love has a huge effect on our lives. I don't know what you are feeling right now, but I know how it felt for me.

Sad, alone, and angry, the pain wouldn't go away. They say time heals, and I suppose it does. But never fully.

We never realise what we have until it's gone, do we? What we should have said was how we felt.

So if I could give you that one wish, what would you ask for right now? Would it be a second chance? To be able to tell them how much you love them? To say you're sorry?

But suppose I really could give you that second chance? I know you are probably thinking that I'm crazy at this point; that it's impossible.

But just suppose I could. A chance to be able to speak to them, walk with them, laugh, and cry with them?

It is not an image of you being there, it is you actually being there with them. And it will be very emotional. You will cry and feel sadness, but it WILL allow you to let go.

I know it is hard to believe, but I am here to tell you it is possible. I know it's possible, because I do it EVERY DAY.

So if you are willing to take a leap of faith, let me take you on this Magical Journey, so you can start living again. Isn't that what they want for us?

Have you ever had a dream and what you experienced was so powerful that you were living that life?

Just suppose there was a way, with the aid of hypnosis and the power of your mind, to be able to open up a doorway into your subconscious to see the people you have lost and talk to them.

I know what you are thinking; that it is impossible. I am here to tell you it is not. Please take the time and read their stories.

The Celestial Connection: A Magical Voyage to Heal the Heart

"In the mystical land of Luminara, a place where the stars shone brighter than anywhere else, there was a secret art known as Stellar Soul Healing.

"This ancient practice allowed one to journey beyond the physical realm, unlocking the mysteries of the mind to mend the wounds left by loss and grief.

"Aria, a young healer in Luminara, had a unique gift. She could hear the whispers of the stars, their celestial melodies guiding her path.

"When her beloved sister, Lyra, passed away, Aria's heart shattered into a thousand pieces, leaving her with a deep, unrelenting sorrow. In her darkest moments, she longed to find solace and to heal her broken heart.

"One starry night, as Aria gazed at the heavens, a brilliant shooting star streaked across the sky, leaving a trail of sparkling stardust.

"Entranced, she followed the shimmering trail to a hidden grove, where she discovered an ancient, celestial tome. This was the Book of Stellar Soul Healing, a sacred text containing the wisdom of the stars.

"As Aria immersed herself in the book's teachings, she discovered that the connection between the living and the departed was not severed, but instead transcended time and space. The key to healing her heartache lay within the mysteries of the mind and the power of the stars.

"With newfound determination, Aria embarked on a magical voyage to the Celestial Realm, guided by the melodies of the stars. As she journeyed through the cosmos, she encountered wondrous beings and celestial landscapes, each reflecting her inner emotions and the memories she held dear.

"In the heart of the Celestial Realm, Aria found the Garden of Remembrance, a radiant haven where the souls of the departed could reunite with their loved ones.

"There, among the blossoms of ethereal starflowers, she found Lyra, her sister's luminous spirit waiting to embrace her.

"As Aria and Lyra reunited, their love transcended the boundaries of the physical world, soothing the pain that had engulfed Aria's heart. The sisters shared stories and laughter, their celestial connection mending the wounds left by loss and grief.

"As their time in the Garden of Remembrance drew to a close, Lyra bestowed upon Aria a sacred gift: a gleaming star crystal that held the essence of their bond. With this treasure, Aria would always carry a piece of her sister's love and the knowledge that their connection was eternal.

"Aria returned to Luminara, her heart lighter and filled with newfound hope. She dedicated her life to sharing the magic of Stellar Soul Healing, guiding others on their celestial voyages to heal the heartache left by the loss of their loved ones.

"As a result, Luminara's star knowledge kept shining, serving as a reminder of the strength of love and the indestructible ties that bind us all across space and time."

The fictional works I've given are meant to arouse a feeling of awe and enchantment. Although the story is fiction, it does touch on topics that have real-world applications, including the significance of self-discovery and the strength of the mind.

The story's central ideas can motivate us to investigate the possibilities of our own minds and the effects that our thoughts and feelings can have on our wellbeing, even though the magical elements are fictional.

PART THREE

Their Stories

A Magical Story of Belief.

"Once upon a time, in a land far, far away, there was a young girl named Aurora who had been suffering from a rare and incurable disease for years.

"Despite countless visits to doctors and healers, nothing seemed to alleviate her pain or slow the progression of her illness.

"One day, as she lay in her bed feeling hopeless and defeated, she heard a soft whisper in her ear. "Believe," it said. "Believe in the power of your own mind to heal your body."

"Aurora was sceptical at first, but as the voice continued to urge her to trust in her own abilities, she began to feel a spark of hope within her. She closed her eyes and focused all her energy on believing that she was capable of healing herself through the power of her mind.

"As the days went by, Aurora's belief grew stronger and stronger. She visualised her body becoming stronger and healthier, and she felt a sense of peace and calm within her that she had never experienced before.

"One morning, as she woke up, she felt a strange tingling sensation throughout her body. At first, she was afraid that her disease was getting worse, but then she realised that it was something different. It was a feeling of energy and vitality that she had never felt before.

"As she got out of bed and looked in the mirror, she couldn't believe what she saw. Her skin, once sallow and pale, was now glowing a vibrant, healthy colour. Her eyes, once tired and dull, now sparkled with life and energy.

"Aurora knew that she had done it. She had healed herself through the power of her own mind and the strength of her belief. From that day forward, she lived every moment of her life with a newfound sense of purpose and passion, knowing that anything was possible as long as she believed in herself."

Elaine's Story

Elaine lost her father at the beginning of 2019. Her story is told from the heart. All she wanted was to dance with her father again and so she did.

"I have known Geoff for many years; mainly through his marriage to my cousin Jackie. We were close friends until my husband and I moved abroad in the mid-80s.

"Even though there were occasional letters and telephone calls at the beginning, we seemed to drift apart and it was therefore extra special when Geoff phoned me after my father had passed away at the beginning of 2019.

"We chatted for a while, and I told him how he had died in his sleep in the hospital and I never got the chance to say goodbye; and the guilt I felt that he had left this world alone.

"We talked for ages and I mentioned a song I had heard recently called 'Dance with my Father Again' and how I wished I could have just one more 'dance' with him and tell him how much I love him and miss him.

"A few weeks later, Geoff phoned again. He was coming to my neck of the woods for a conference and wanted to know if we could meet up. Instead of just 'meeting up' I invited Geoff to stay – and he did.

"It was a fabulous couple of days – catching up and sharing photographs of our children, and our grandchildren. Geoff also talked about Hypnotherapy and I half-jokingly asked if I could have a session with him. Of course, he said yes.

"He sat me in a comfortable chair, told me to close my eyes and to imagine a set of stairs and to tell him if they were going up or down.

"I told him they were 'going up'. He asked me to walk up the stairs and that there would be a door at the top. As I walked, Geoff quietly counted from one to ten. I learned afterwards that this counting was increasing the depth of the trance he was putting me under.

"He asked me questions about the door: What colour it was; heavy or light; panelled or flat; old or new.

Again, with every answer I was giving him, I was going deeper and deeper and deeper.

"We then got to the door. It was closed, with light, like sunshine, shining through the top and the sides. Geoff told me to open the door and that I would be taken to a beautiful magical place. He told me there would be a pathway, which I was to follow and to tell him where I was and what I was seeing.

"I was in a park – or a field – with a narrow stream running from one side to the other. On the bank of the stream stood my entire family: husband, children with their spouses and grandchildren. Everyone standing before me – not saying anything.

"Geoff then asked me what else I could see. As I looked to the left, there was a huge tree and standing beneath the tree was my father. I ran to him and threw my arms around his neck, hugging him so tightly as he hugged me back just as tightly.

"I was sobbing, heart-breaking and crying. I kept telling him how much I loved him and missed him –

and that I was so sorry I hadn't been there with him at the end.

"He didn't say anything, but just feeling his arms around me again was all I needed. We stayed like that for a while – just standing together under that beautiful tree - me stroking his back, sobbing uncontrollably – and without him saying anything, I felt his love again, which I had needed so badly.

"I remember Geoff bringing me tissues and telling me it was time to say goodbye. He brought me back through the same process he had used to take me to my father – only in reverse.

"This happened over three years ago, but I can still see that 'picture' so clearly and I can still feel my father's arms around me.

"Thank you, Geoff. You will never know how much you gave me that day, giving me the chance to 'Dance with my Father' again."

"If I could steal one final glance, one final step

> ***One final dance with him***
> ***I'd play a song that would***
> ***never ever end***
> ***'Cause I'd love, love, love***
> ***to dance with my father***
> ***again."***
>
> *Dance with My Father"*
> *by Luther Vandross*

On reading Elaine's story I want you, the reader, to try to put yourself in her shoes and visualise what she must have been going through.

Once you have done that, I want you to write down in your own words what you went through and how you felt when you lost a loved one. Doing so will make it easier for you to let go of the past.

I know what it's like to lose someone close to you, holding onto that grief and how it tears you apart. However, rather than honouring a death, we should be welcoming the life that was lost.

It's natural to withdraw in times of sorrow, but you can't afford to because others depend on you.

So now it's time to write your story and remember you are not alone...

Reliving The Past

The following are three stories, all of which can be found in Chapters of my first book; "Are You Reliving Someone Else's Life?"

Tony is 17 years old, Dianne is 31, and James is 33.

It's likely that you're curious about the motivation behind my decision to include it in my third book.

I believe it is essential for you to have an understanding of how a person's heart may be healed by viewing the people they have lost

Tony's Story

This is Tony's story, taken from my first book: Are You Reliving Someone Else's Life? The Loveday Method

Because of the profound impact, it has had on Tony's life I felt the need to write this again, to show you that the changes can be quite remarkable.

"Due to losing my nana very recently, I wanted to see her. Geof started by letting me picture stairs; they were my nana's stairs.

"With every step, I went deeper into the trance, until I reached the top. A new, shiny, black door presented itself. I took a deep breath and with Geof's guidance, I walked through. I was met on a warm summer morning, on top of a mountain with a beautiful sunrise in the distance. I could feel the grass on my feet and I was at peace. Geof then helped me find the path, a wooden decked path that led me to a lake with a waterfall to my left and endless green fields and the sunrise to my right.

"As I was standing there I saw a light, and out of it came my nana, my granddad and their beloved dog Lucy. I was in shock. There stood in front of me were my granddad who passed away 21 years ago, my nana who I've recently lost, and the family dog from my childhood. They looked alive, happy, well and at peace.

My nana put her hands out to me and I held her and felt an overwhelming sense of relief and warmth. The first thing I said when I lost her was that I needed to feel her hands, and she knew that. I told her that it was okay, and to forgive her for any emotions she has passed down.

"Then to my granddad, I forgave him for anything he passed down to me and told him it was okay. He shook my hand and rested his hand on the shoulder that had carried my nanas coffin. The weight that I had previously felt had been lifted. I felt so much lighter. I gave them both a hug and was then joined by my mum and sister. We were all reunited.

"When it was time to leave, with Lucy the dog by their side, they turned around and walked into the light. Before they did, my nana turned around to me and nodded at me, letting me know it was all going to be okay. It was the most incredible and fulfilling experience I have ever had in my life.

"Geof unlocked the door for me and pulled down the barriers to the place where my nana and grandad could contact me, and see me. This has changed how I feel about her passing, and I am happy she's at rest with my granddad. I have been assured of that now."

Tony is now doing amazing. He is a qualified lifeguard doing shifts after school, he is learning to drive, is back seeing his dad again, and going to the gym.

Tony came to see me on 2nd August 2022. Six months have passed.

I need to mention Tony was booked in for six sessions; unfortunately, he only had two.

I contacted Tony's mum because I felt he needed to complete the programme, but because he was doing so well they decided he didn't need them at that time. I felt that was a wrong decision

It's very much like a course of antibiotics. You may feel better after two days but it is so important you complete the course.

But the story doesn't end there. I received a text from Tony's mum recently saying he'd lost his grandfather and that he needs my help. That's both grandparents he'd lost in seven months.

It is crucial to emphasize once again that completing all six sessions is essential for the program to be effective. Currently, it has been eleven months since Tony's last session, and today, on Friday, May 26th, 2023, he has decided to return to me to complete the remaining sessions. This decision comes after the passing of his grandfather, which has likely had a significant impact on Tony's emotional well-being.

"Today's session with Geoff was incredible. The journey I went on surprised both of us! Geoff started by putting me under; feeling energy raising my hands and my eyelids closing, going deeper by the second. I was then asked to visualise a set of stairs; they were purple. As Geoff counted to ten, I walked up the stairs. I was then greeted by a door, a grand door, old and a mesmerising golden colour.

"Geoff explained to me that through this door there would be a library. As Geoff guided me through the door, I was greeted with a vast room, filled with bookshelves on either side of me. It was dissimilar to any other library I had seen before. The books on the shelves were old, almost ancient. This library had stood here for a very long time.

"Geoff then asked if I could see a chair. I looked straight ahead of me to discover a grand wooden chair, huge in size, with beautiful patterns carved into the wood. Geoff explained to me that this was not any ordinary chair; this chair would take me on a journey through time. He explained that I was going to be transported to a place. With Geoff's guidance, I sat in the chair and with one tap on my forehead, my surroundings changed.

I was on a beach; it was incredibly familiar to me the second I came to my senses. It was Bencllech Beach in Anglesey, a place of many fond memories from my childhood. I was walking with someone who is very close to my heart, my Grandfather, one of the only people who had been a constant since meeting them. Someone who put themselves before me and always made it their priority to help me to battle my traumas, from past to present.

"We were holding hands. Geoff told me to continue walking, looking out at the beautiful sunset. As I walked, I felt an incredible change from my 18-year-old self. I felt physical and mental changes. A change of energy inside of me, and a change in the way I thought.

"I also felt a difference in my hand and the hand that I was holding. As I looked down at myself, I had again gone back in time. I was 7 years old. I turned to my left to be greeted by my grandfather, who passed away in late 2022. I was in shock, but it felt so normal.

"As we walked, Geoff asked me if I could forgive him. I told him that I can no longer hold onto any pain that I am feeling that he experienced in his life. I watched a cloud of dark energy leave myself and my grandfather, followed by a vivid golden light surrounding and entering us both. I felt the change in myself instantly.

"After this, I felt myself change back into my 18-year-old self. Geoff asked me if anyone else stood with me and my grandfather, and as I turned, there stood was my 7-year-old self, looking up at me and my grandfather. I hugged him, put my hands on his shoulders and forgave him. Again, dark energy left us both, with that golden light following. I told him to be strong and to be grateful for everyone around him.

"Geoff then told me that it was time to live the life of a past relative. With another touch on my forehead, I left the familiar beach to be greeted by an equally familiar room. Geoff asked me to look around and describe the room in the best way possible.

"I was sat on a throne, in a grand room, with a marble floor, grand paintings on the wall, and a breathtaking view greeting me; a beaming sun and a beautiful view of the sea in the distance.

"I was then asked to describe what I was wearing. I had golden buckled shoes, and a grand robe around me. I felt powerful, but so hollow inside. Geoff then asked if I was accompanied in the room. I was not, however, I could feel the presence of people significant to me in this house.

"I knew straight away that it was my family; and as soon as I thought of them, they came through the door. I had a wife, with brown hair and brown eyes and two children, a boy of 9 and a girl of 7. I saw the pain in their eyes and a touch of fear. However, I could feel a

burning sensation of love towards me that I could just not let in.

"I felt a painful need for this love, but I was scared that if I accepted it, I would lose the power and pride that I had worked so hard to gain. I was torturing myself. I then felt myself change to my 18-year-old self, looking at this disjointed family. My ancestor stood tall, with long brown hair and a powerful stance. However, he was completely empty, isolated on an island alone, surrounded by a sea of love, too scared to swim.

"With Geoff's guidance, I forgave my ancestor for the feelings I inherited from him, as they are not mine, and I could no longer hold onto them. As I did, I watched a dark ball of black energy leave him, and I. could see a visible change in his face and posture. Then, a glistening ball of light came down from the skies and entered our bodies.

"After this, my ancestor embraced his wife, and his two children. This filled me with happiness and love, a family who could finally be together, As the wife and 2 children looked at me, I felt immense radiations of love and thankfulness coming from them. I knew that myself and my ancestor had learnt to accept love and let go of any pride that was stopping us from doing so. With a nod of my ancestor's head and a tap on the forehead from Geoff, I left this place.

"I was greeted by the library again, and I sat in the chair. Geoff then asked me if any books stood out or presented themselves to me. A red book appeared in my hands; it had a blank cover. Geoff asked me to start flicking through the pages and see if anything stood out to me. I stopped on a page that read; "love is something that we must use."

"I continued to flick through the pages; another page stated that pride should not be the death of you. I finally reached a page with a picture of the beach. Geoff asked me to look at the picture, and with a tap on my forehead, I was there. Back on the beach, sat alone, watching the great orange sun begin to hide behind the clouds.

"I felt a sense of peace, learning so many valuable lessons about myself on my journey. I felt a physical difference inside of me, an energy that was not there before.

"Geoff then asked me if anyone was with me and as I turned, my grandfather showed himself. We sat in silence, with his arm around me, watching the sun go down together. This was emotional for me. My grandfather was the one person in my life who never gave up on me, no matter the circumstance. The warmth and love I felt from him were breath-taking, taking me back to my childhood.

"As the sun finally went to sleep, and the sky grew darker, my grandfather stood. With an unforgettable smile on his face and a twinkle in his eyes, he hugged me. He held my face and told me he was eternally proud, and that he would always be with me. He then turned and walked into a blinding golden light returning to his rest.

Geoff then brought me back, and we were both so surprised by how much the life and feelings of my ancestor correlated with those of mine. This session has changed the way that I think about myself and how I feel internally. I am no longer scared to be alone, because I am not. My grandparents are always with me, and I'm sure that my ancestor will now be too.

What I want you, the reader, to do is write down what you think Tony went through and where the suffering originated in his life.

I also want you to consider whether or not there is a correlation between how you were raised and the things that you went through as a youngster and how it has impacted your life today.

So now it's time to write your story; and remember, you are not alone...

Dianne's Story

Diane was 31 when she came to see me. She suffered from depression, anxiety, sadness and panic attacks. She had a fear of being pregnant but wanted a child so desperately. But she could not conceive as she never got over the passing of her father.

Dianne's First Session.

"My first session was everything I hoped it would be. I had hoped for some kind of connection to my subconscious, which is exactly what happened. I had hoped even more for some kind of 'sign' that I was on

the right track, that I was doing the right thing. I didn't dare hope for a connection to my dad, who passed away seven years ago, that would have been too big of a wish. But that's exactly what I got, and not in a "medium" type way.

"Geof guided me into hypnosis where I felt safe and comfortable and relaxed. When Geof told me that when he tapped my left hand there would be someone waiting for me and I would know and see them instantly, as soon as he tapped my hand I felt him. My dad's presence was there, which I have been missing since he left this life.

"It's not like we were speaking as we would have done when he was living, but I could feel his love and his smile. My dad was my best friend, but he had suffered on and off throughout his life from depression, which I undoubtedly absorbed as a child. Geof guided me to return to my dad the pain which was his and not mine.

"I returned that pain to him with love and understanding. With empathy, because I know that pain wasn't his either, someone gave it to him.

"Tears streamed down my face continuously, sometimes sobbing as the blocked emotion left my body. The tears were a mix – some sad tears because of how much I had missed him, but mostly happy joyous tears that I was 'seeing' him again, rather than that I was feeling him again. I felt the tears purging all this emotion out of me.

"When I didn't think the experience could get any more emotional or any more transcendent, Geof quietly asked me if there was anyone else there with my Dad. I told him there was but they were small and I couldn't make out who it was. I soon realised it was a child or a baby. There seemed to be a lightness around this child and as I got closer to them I realised it was my child - my future child, not yet born, not yet even conceived.

"Yes, I know – my mind is blown! I have suffered from fertility issues for some years and am booked in to start IVF in the coming months. Since my Dad died, one of the things which made me very sad was the thought that my future children would never know their granddad – what a cool, funny, caring, kind, soft, man he was. It hurt my heart that they would only know him through photographs and stories, that they wouldn't truly feel his love, which is the most powerful love I have ever experienced.

"When I saw my dad with this child, it was as if he was telling me that the baby I will one day be blessed with was with him now, as we speak, waiting for it's time to come here, to this life. It's like he was reassuring me that my worst fear was redundant because my future child came from him and was sent by him. As I write this now I can picture one day telling my kid this story when they're old enough to understand.

"Also, every time I have recounted this story so far I've accidentally said 'him' when referring to the baby. I wonder if I'll have a boy. If I do, I had already thought about naming him after his amazing granddad, Edward, but now I definitely will be – whenever his granddad Eddie sends him."

I want you, the reader, to look into Dianne's thoughts and see where her journey led her and how she was able to release her sorrow and let go by taking her to see her father who had passed away her best friend.

The next step is for you to write down how you would react if you were suddenly able to see the people who you have loved but lost.

So now it's time to write your story and remember you are not alone...

James' Story

James came to see me on the 22nd of October 2022. His initial motivation for coming to see me was because he had resorted to alcohol as a way of avoiding his troubles and his life since he was suffering from depression, stress, tension, dissatisfaction, and the dread of being judged.

James, who is now 33 years old, suffered the loss of his brother, who took his own life at the age of 26, and has never fully recovered from the loss

He is now a happily married father of a beautiful son.

Another level, by James

"It is now 23rd February 2023.

"On this Saturday morning, the usual nervousness was setting in before my session with Geoff. I had spoken to Geof about my previous urges with alcohol and how I was trying to keep them at bay.

"The session began with the usual process of lowering my level of consciousness. Once I was in a deep state, I could see my urges with alcohol as a negative force leaving my body. These were honed in on in a series of cleansing actions. At first, my arm raised 100% to represent my connection with alcohol and then 75%, 50%, and 25% and then no matter how hard I tried to lift my arm I couldn't move it as the urges were being purged.

"Once this was complete, Geof asked me to visualise a set of stairs. A dark set of concrete stairs that led downwards appeared... There was an old black door at the bottom. I was guided through to the other side.

"This was a safe space in between worlds, Geof asked me to take myself back to the person closest linked to my alcohol issues... not long after this my grandfather

appeared (who died of alcoholism). I spoke with him and told him I could no longer live his life any more, I needed to give these mistakes and urges back to him. Dark energy began to leave my body and both I and my grandfather were cleansed by a ray of golden light.

"It was extremely emotional seeing my grandfather, a person who I had never actually met as he died before I was born. The connection and sense of love were so real.

"My grandfather then left via a ball of light. Geof then asked me to go back further into where or where my grandfather got his alcohol problems from.

"It was extremely foggy at first but then a shelter of some sort appeared. There was a group of around 30 men looking towards one man standing on a podium. The person who I had gone back in time to was a man in his late 20s.

"The men were all screaming in anger, fear and frustration. Geof probed asking, what were the men screaming about – food, medicine and water. There was a disease of the lungs affecting the people of this place.

This man had a wife and two girls that were sick and needed help.

"As this time passed it became evident that only 5 of the 30 men would get the provisions they needed and the person I was inhabiting was turned away.

"I literally felt every single drop of emotion that this man was feeling; that he was going to lose his family, his wife and two daughters. They would all die and this was a stark realisation.

"At this point the man didn't go home to comfort his family, he travelled to a local inn and began to get blind drunk. He ran away from his family and left them and numbed the pain with alcohol.

"I confronted this person and explained that I could no longer live his life. I'm not going to use alcohol as a crutch to escape issues in my life.

"You can see the connection between his grandfather who died from alcohol, whom he had never met, who died before he was born. and how he was living out his grandfather's life."

On reading his story it appears that it has been passed down through his genes.

That it is not his fault and that he is not to blame. And he is reliving someone else's life.

Contact with the Dead

"I first approached Geof in late 2022 due to suffering from anxiety, depression and alcoholism. I had never considered hypnotherapy as a course of treatment in the past so this was a new experience to me.

"During my consultation with Geoff he asked me about a wide range of things from diet, general lifestyle and family members that had passed on. Even pets.

"My brother had taken his own life seven years ago which was an extremely traumatic event, there were lots of emotions buried deep inside me around this.

"I had a total of 6 sessions with Geof, which I can only describe as completely and utterly mind blowing!

"During one of the sessions, I travelled up a set of golden stairs into the open universe. Then exploring the cosmos and finding myself on an island with nothing but stars above me.

"Geof guided me down a path, past a waterfall and down to a small lake. My brother, who had passed on, was waiting there for me.

"The first thing he said was, "alright mate!" At this point, I completely broke down and tears were streaming down my face. It was so good catching up with him and having the conversations that I thought I had missed the chance on!

"He was asking about his two sons and how they were, asking about my mother and sisters. It was such an amazing experience. We talked for a good while until he hugged me and left, returning to the cosmos.

"Meeting my brother again under hypnosis brought some element of closure to me. It gave me an opportunity to tell him I loved him one last time.

"In another session, I was reunited with my grandparents who told me to "Stop being daft!" referring to my recent sadness.

"These were my grandparents on my mother's side. They had both died before I was born. Again this was an insane experience! Meeting family and having conversations with them as if they were right in front of me.

"They were asking about my mother and other family members. They let me know that I was loved by them and all of my family.

"I struggled to comprehend some of the sessions but ultimately felt so much comfort and relief having met family that had passed on. It gave me a sense of hope that I had never had before, that there is something more than this reality.

"I'll always be grateful to Geof for being the person who let me speak with my brother one last time."

On reading, you will see James's reaction about his extraordinary experience. Try to imagine yourself in James' position and consider your response.

So now it's time to write your story and remember you are not alone...

Magical Journey with Sarah.

This reminds me of another story from my time spent teaching hypnotherapy in schools. The head teacher and I were both seated around a table with around 10 other teachers.

One of the teachers said she would love to be hypnotised but she didn't think she could be. I replied "You think?"

I love a challenge so in front of all these teachers I got her into a very deep trance. Bear in mind, I knew nothing about this lady. I got here to picture a set of stairs. When you do nod your head, do the stairs go up or down?

"Up", she replied.

"In a moment I will count from 1 to 10. Each number I count will be a step you take at the top of the stairs you will see a door." I started to count, and on the count of ten I said, "You can see a door? Can you see the door?"

"Yes", she replied.

You have to understand, this lady believed that everything she saw she was making up, so with all the answers she was giving me she was being sarcastic. That's okay, because everything I was saying to her was sending her deeper.

So let's see what happened.

"Tell me the colour of the door."
"Brown", she replied.
"Is it heavy or light, heavy panelled or flat?"
"Flat."

I repeated it, saying "So it is heavy-panelled and flat. Is that right?" She replied with a yes.

"In a moment you will open that door and the door will follow you wherever you go. If you feel uncomfortable in any way you can turn around, open the door, walk through and close the door. Any worries or fears will melt away. Just nod your head if you understand and accept", I told her.

She nodded.

I told her to open the door, and she replied that it's locked. I knew it was locked. I told her to look for a key on the floor. "Can you see it?"

"Yes", she replied.

"Open the door walkthrough and close the door behind you. Is it daytime or night-time?" I asked.

"Night time."

"Are you inside or outside?"

"Outside."

"With someone or on your own?"

"On my own."

"Where are you?"

"On a football pitch."

"Isn't it dark?"

"The lights are on."

"Wow", I replied, "you have an answer for everything.

Look down at your feet and tell me what you see."

"Slippers."

"Scan your body and tell me what you have on."

"Dressing gown."

"How old are you?"

"Ten."

"What is a little girl of ten doing on a football pitch in the middle of the night?"

"I don't know."

"Of course you do", I told her. "So you are a ten-year-old little girl at night on a football pitch and wearing slippers and a dressing gown the lights are on. Why?"

"I don't know Geof", she replied.

"Of course, you do", I told her again. I want you to look for something that you are connected to as to why you are there."

"I see a golden vase at the other end of the football pitch."

"So go to the other end of the football pitch. What do you think you should do?"

"I think I should look in the vase."

"You are so nosey I think you should. What can you see?"

"A red velvet lining."

"What does it mean?"

"I don't know."

"Yes you do. You are a ten-year-old girl on a football pitch at night and wearing slippers and a dressing gown. The lights are on. You see a vase at the other end of the football pitch made of gold. You look inside and see red velvet lining. Why?"

Now she is getting angry. "I don't know. I won't tell you again, Geof."

I keep pushing her.

"So you are a ten-year-old girl on a football pitch at night and wearing slippers and a dressing gown. The lights are on. You see a vase at the other end of the football pitch made of gold. You look inside and see red velvet lining. Why?"

She screams at me.

"Look in the vase again, what do you see?"
"Red velvet lining."
"What are you feeling Sarah?"

She then burst into tears.

"Why are you crying?" I asked.
"I really don't know", she said. "I know that I am in a room full of teachers, but I am this ten-year-old little

girl on a football pitch who has no idea why I am here and I'm so confused. And I do not cry."

"I want you now to look for something else about why you are there", I told her.

"I see my children at the other end of the football pitch."

"Go to the other end of the football pitch. Do you love your children?"

"Yes."

"What does it mean?"

"I don't know."

"Of course you do."

You have to understand, at this point I have no idea where this journey will take her. But you are about to find out.

"So you are a ten-year-old little girl at night on a football pitch", I repeated. "The lights are on, you are wearing slippers and a dressing gown. You see a vase at the other end of the football pitch made of gold. You look inside and see red velvet lining. You see your children at the end of the football pitch. Why?"

"I really don't know, Geof."

"When I touch you on the forehead you will."

I touch her on the forehead and say "Now you remember?"

She hesitates to say no.

"Oh my goodness I do."
"You are there now, is it daytime or night-time?"
"Daytime."
"Inside or outside."
"Outside."
"With someone or on your own?"
"With someone."
"Who are you with?"
"I am with my grandmother. Every Saturday, I would visit my grandmother, whose house overlooked the main football stadium, and we would watch the game together."
"What do you have on?"
"Slippers and a dressing gown."
"What is your grandmother wearing?"
"A dressing gown made of red velvet."
"Sarah, you're not telling me everything."
"I am."

"YOU ARE NOT. Why were you crying and why were you so emotional?"

"Oh my goodness, now I remember being sad and disappointed when my grandmother died and I realised she would never see her grandchildren."

"You miss your Grandmother, don't you?"

"Yes."

"She has never left your side and has always kept a close watch on you. When you were upset, she comforted you by wiping away your tears, and when you were happy, she danced with you. Would you like to see her?"

"Yes",

"She's over there."

At that moment her Grandmother appeared in front of her.

She burst into tears. She hugged her grandmother, and she told her that she was so proud of her.

"I think you should introduce your grandmother to your children", I told her.

And she saw her Grandmother playing with her children. How amazing is that and what an incredible gift she was given!

The head teacher had to leave the room because she was so emotional, as were the other teachers. We brought Sarah back into the room.

Everyone in the room couldn't believe what happened. What I didn't realise was that Sarah was the Deputy Head.

Sarah called me two days later to tell me she had realised what the vase meant. After her grandmother passed away, her body was cremated, and her grandfather stored the ashes of her grandmother in a vase that was made of gold.

A second chance has been given to Sarah to visit and speak with her grandmother.

After reading the story of Sarah you will begin to realise the sadness she was holding onto was locked away inside her mind eventually the sadness that she felt regarding her grandmother may have created a problem later in life.

Now, please take a moment to examine your thoughts.

Is there an unseen influence that you cannot see that is contributing to how miserable and isolated you feel?

Is there something that is preventing you from enjoying your life to the fullest?

So now it's time to write your story and remember you are not alone...

Amy's Story

I have been monitoring Amy over the course of around 12 months.

"It has been 6 weeks since my appointments finished and I have been doing great. Happiness was the main goal, followed by weight loss and I have definitely achieved both. I lost a further 12 pounds in January, I'm eating better and I am a regular gym member.

"I am very clear-minded now about the result I want to achieve and I don't think I would have got there without my sessions. I am now down a dress size also which is amazing.

"I feel that since my appointments, my anxiety has lessened and I am doing things that usually I would have thought twice about, such as going into an unknown environment and pushing myself, like the gym.

"I want to move more and incorporate exercise into my daily life which before my sessions, used to fill me with dread. I am excited to see how this year plays out

because overall I am feeling positive and really want to make this year mine."

"Can you communicate with the dead?"

"When checking in recently Geof mentioned to me that he had started writing a new book. The title was what caught me off guard and it is an interesting question/subject. I am a sceptic but having experienced this myself in my sessions I can confirm that yes you can communicate with the dead.

"In my sessions, the two main loved ones who came through to me and guided me were my Nan and also my Uncle. Some of my sessions even took Geof by surprise as to where we ended up because I was being guided to places that were out of the norm. It is a feeling that can't really be explained but only experienced.

"Both encounters for me were unreal and magical. Not many people get to have this experience and it isn't like going to see a psychic, this is getting to touch your loved ones, hug them and feel that connection again, something completely different.

"Over a few sessions, I had different encounters, one being by my uncle's graveside and then suddenly he appeared behind it, talking to me and giving me advice. I was only young when he passed so I was able to say goodbye to him in a way I always wished I could.

"Another encounter with my Nan I had was sitting on a bench with her and just having a moment to ourselves, everything felt calm and everything seemed to slow down. Holding her hand as we sat is something I won't forget.

"She told me to find my necklace in one of our sessions; this was a necklace she had engraved before she died so it could be passed to me on my 18th birthday because she knew she wouldn't be here for it.

"I went home and couldn't find the necklace, then suddenly when I was sitting on my bed alone in my thoughts, my little girl Grace came into my room, "Look what I found mummy". It was my necklace.

"I didn't ask her to look for it, and I didn't actually mention it to anyone, but here she was with the one *thing I couldn't find. I burst into tears because I knew this wasn't a coincidence, it was my Nan."*

What an amazing journey Amy went on. I want you to examine her life to see how remembering the individuals we've lost can help us move on with our lives and find peace.

Think about what it would be like to be in Amy's place and then tell me how you would respond.

So now it's time to write your story and remember you are not alone...

Unknown's Story

This is a lady who has lost her father and is suffering from despair, anxiety, and grief. It's been almost 5 years since she came to visit me, and at the time, she was also scheduled for a hysterectomy.

"Hi Geoff. Sorry, it's taken so long! Also please amend anything that I haven't spelt correctly or isn't grammatically correct!

"When I first booked my sessions with Geoff, I had no idea what to expect but was completely open-minded.

My husband found him on the Internet and we thought as a last resort to give hypnotherapy a try.

"After giving birth to my son, which was extremely traumatic and ended in an emergency caesarean. I experienced pain and bled every day for 2 years, and the hospital could not tell me why this was happening.

"They decided the best option would be to have a hysterectomy and remove my womb and ovaries.

"I must add that I was feeling exhausted and I had lost my zest for life. I was so tired and wasn't enjoying being a mum as I found everything such a struggle.

"I met Geoff and we started a course of hypnotherapy and kinesiology sessions. I went back throughout my life to uncover buried trauma. I didn't realise that emotions can be trapped in the body and needed to be released.

"Every time I got back home to my husband after a session he would always say I came back a different person! More relaxed, happy and positive!

"I have now cancelled my operation as I am miraculously not in any pain and have stopped bleeding! This is very strange to me and I have no idea how he did it.

"After 6 sessions the bleeding had completely stopped and I wasn't in any pain at all. I didn't need my painkillers anymore and I started to get back to the gym and exercise, having more energy and positivity. It really is a miracle!

"Geoff is such a kind, caring beautiful human being and I am eternally grateful to have found him! Thank you from the bottom of my heart Geoff!

"During some of the sessions, I had with Geoff We worked on forgiveness. Geoff took me into a deep hypnotic state where I was able to meet up with my dad, who had passed away many years ago.

"I remember this experience vividly and it was extremely powerful and emotional.

"My dad was walking towards me and he looked healthy and happy and he was smiling at me from ear to ear. We held hands and he said he was sorry for all the pain and hurt he had caused.

"I forgave him and cried because I knew he was now at peace and all of my anger disappeared. He walked away and I watched him go. It was so lovely to see him again and to remember his face as I had blocked out trying to remember him as it was too painful.

"My memory of my dad is one of peace and forgiveness now and I can look back without being angry at him anymore. Geoff is just magical and I can't thank him enough."

You have read the stories they wrote in their own words and the journey that they went on. Just reading it, it is hard to believe unless you have experienced the journey yourself.

Was it real? Did they really see their ancestors? Did they make it up? And does it really matter?

The only thing that matters now is how they are feeling. I hope you can see how powerful this is.

After reading her story and observing the changes in both her mental and physical state, do you believe it is possible that the body can be healed through the strength of the mind?

Regardless of your present conditions, do you have the ability to repair your body using only the strength of your mind?

Never lose hope; miracles occur every day.

So now it's time to write your story and remember you are not alone...

Daniel's Story

First Session

"Days before, there's an intense apprehension, a low-level fear.

"What am I about to get myself into? Will it be too much to bear witness to? Will I cope? This wasn't my first rodeo with therapy so I wasn't completely in the dark. However, I knew that hypnoanalysis was and could be a far more direct line of enquiry.

"Session one begins, and me and Geoff convene over zoom, which to my amazement works far better than I had expected. I had been very used to face-to-face therapy.

"Geoff puts me under and we head inside. He guides me gently down deeper and deeper into a relaxed state and then proceeds to tell me that someone will appear in front of you. Who is it? This proceeds to happen over and over again until no one else appears.

"Person after person who has had an impact on my life in ways I was consciously or unconsciously aware of. Mantras are repeated and energies good and bad are released and or reabsorbed.

"Trust in what appears is key, I begin to learn during this session. I am aware of what's happening but I am nonetheless amazed by the range of feelings and emotions that are being covered during the session.

"The session comes to an end. What feels like hours has been completed in forty minutes or less, Geoff tells me. In the immediate aftermath, I felt a psychological lifting of weight off my shoulders. The days after I am exhausted and feelings and emotions come to the surface, which, like an illness, have to come through to get to the potential on the other side.

"Geoff checks in with me on day two to console me from my concerns.

"A few more days pass and I feel the proverbial 'ship has' come out of its first storm. Things have shifted. I am not sure to what degree yet or what that means. But I know I am now better prepared for session two."

Daniel - Session two.

"A week has passed and the intense opening of session one is fading into the background. Grounded again, I become renewed in my conviction to keep with the program and dawning on me now is the anticipation of what's to come from session two.

"Geoff and I meet again over the wires, back into the 'zoom zone'. Geoff informs me that we are going to meet people; potential ancestors from the past. The importance of this can't be understated as Geoff goes on to explain."

'What your carrying in the present isn't necessarily yours to begin with. In fact, it could have come from another lifetime many generations ago.'

"At this point in my 'Journey' I sensed intuitively what he was alluding to. A gut or instinctual feeling that had been with me for most of my life. Something I was holding onto that felt not like mine.

"We have all heard at some point the expression 'It runs in the family.' But what I wasn't expecting was how deep the well could potentially run.

"So session two began much like session one, with Geoff coaxing me deeper and deeper into a relaxed hypnotic state.

"The same script applied: the stairs, then the door, through the door out the other side to someone ready to greet you there. And the same questions:

'Is it daytime or night-time?'
'Are they male or female?'
'What are they wearing?'
'What time have they appeared to you from?'

"As the questions were reeled off by Geoff one by one the picture began to paint in front of me. I knew that my resistance to painting the past was still present with me but unlike session one I asked it to step aside and I promised myself to remain open to what was coming naturally to me.

"Geoff was only asking me questions, he wasn't prompting anything. And so gradually and then all at once a man appeared before me.

"A man from the 1800's. I could picture his face, his dress and even a sense of how he may have walked and talked. Geoff then signalled to me."

'In a moment you are going to feel everything that he felt, everything that he had held onto all his fears, his concerns, his worries, his traumas.....now.'

"And in that moment my chest immediately constricted the dull ache that I recognised in my body was again coming through me through this apparent relative/stranger I had never met. It was uncannily similar the intensity of the feelings to which we both shared.

"Geoff comes in again and says repeats after me: 'I will not and cannot live your life anymore.' He goes on and I repeat back verse after verse and then a releasing of energy from inside back into the light.

"The man steps through an open door and signals back to me, and then we move on again in time to another ancestor.

"And they are there now. 'Is it daytime or night-time?' Geoff continues. A woman begins to appear, this time from the 1400s to my utter disbelief. Her face appears
more and more as we run through the line of enquiry.

"And again Geoff signals me to feel her frustrations and longings. As before they come as firmly as the man from the 1800's. However this time, I feel an even bigger identification with this woman, her life becoming increasingly clearer to me as I sit with her in this brief moment of deep reflection.

"Geoff signals again once more and the mantras and releasing of energy of past burdens take hold of both of us.

"And then before I know it I am beginning the journey back to the surface. On the way, Geoff passes me by an open valley as a gift, a message specifically for me *that only I know what it would mean. Message received and eyes wide open 5,4,3,2,1.*

"Session two comes to an end as quickly as it has begun."

On the 14th of January in 2023, Daniel contacted me. Depression and sadness plagued him throughout his childhood, and he struggled with feelings of abandonment and poor self-esteem as a result. He was mentally bullied in school.

It's amazing how much our beliefs can influence our lives and how closely we hold onto the past that we just can't seem to let go of.

Until about the age of seven, we are programmed to draw on the energy and feelings of other people and latch onto their suffering.

Now I ask you, the reader, are you holding onto the suffering of others? Is your life being controlled by an unseen influence that you can't explain?

You need to search for the answers within yourself.

The question we must ask ourselves is, was it there before you were born and are we reliving someone else's life?

So now it's time to write your story and remember you are not alone...

The Sinking of the Lusitania.

An interesting story. Where do I begin?

Jonathan came to see me on the 7th of January 2023 suffering from depression, anxiety, stress, unhappiness, and guilt.

He is 66 years young, happily married, and has two children and one granddaughter.

The guilt that he has is related to travelling away from home. I asked him if he had one wish, what would it be?

His answer was to enjoy his holiday. It seems so silly, doesn't it? But to him it wasn't, as it was affecting his life, and not only his, but the relationship with his family.

Every time they went away they would always have to come back early because he would have pains in his chest and panic attacks that became so severe they had to return home.

For every problem, there is a solution. We just have to find it.

The big question is where do we look for the answers?

I believe that the answers we are searching for were there long before Jonathan was born. That he was suffering from Transgenerational Trauma.

Transgenerational Trauma is a form of psychological trauma that is passed down from one generation to the next.

So how is it possible that something that happened 100 years ago, or 200/300/1000 years ago is causing the problem in Jonathan's life today and that he is reliving his ancestor's life?

Hopefully, I may give you an insight into why and how this is possible.

Let me drift away from the story just for a moment. And I would like to ask the readers a question.

Q. Would you believe that something that happened 100, 200, 500, 1000, or 10000 years ago is affecting your life today?

I know it is difficult to believe. But bear with me for the moment. We know that cancer and diabetes can be passed down from one generation to the next.

What about the misery, anxiety, and despair that our parents' great, great, grandparents experienced in their lives? Is it possible that we are holding onto their suffering?

Q. Who do you look like, your mum or your dad?

There will be similarities because your DNA is passed down from your parents to you. What about your grandparent's DNA is it also passed down from your grandparents to your parents to you, or your great-grandparent's DNA from your grandparents to your parents to you?

Epigenetics states it can go back over at least 14 generations. But do we really know how far it can go back?

There is an invisible force that is causing so much unhappiness in the world today; it is causing depression, anxiety, stress, fear and many other issues.

It is an epidemic affecting many people worldwide who have no idea where to get help.

And so The Loveday Method was formed.

The Loveday Method is a sophisticated means of achieving time travel through the mind in order to access hidden memories within the DNA responsible for generational trauma in order to unlock the shackles your ancestral traumas hold over you.

And that you are Reliving Someone Else's Life.

Now let us get back to Jonathan's story…

It starts with me putting Jonathan into a very deep trance. I take him to the Akashic Library, the Library of

Life. In the library, there are many books he talks to me under hypnosis explaining exactly what he sees.

He tells me he sees a chair, a very old red leather chair he described in detail. I get him to sit in the chair and tell him that he will be transported through time to many generations before he was born where he will relive an ancestor's life whether it will be male or female, and where the fear that Jonathan is holding onto originated.

Once sitting in the chair it took him back to 1915, he became his great-great-grandfather, and he then explained to me in detail the experience he was feeling and reliving.

He told me he was dressed in a sailor's uniform and was looking forward to seeing his family who he missed so much.

He was sad that he had been away from home and his family for far too long and was depressed because of it.

He told me the date was May 1st 1915, and he was on pier 54, travelling from New York to Liverpool on the Lusitania.

The RMS Lusitania was a UK-registered ocean liner that made regular trips across the Atlantic at the time.

Unbeknown to him, he will never see his family again. On the 7th of May 1915, the Lusitania was torpedoed by an imperial German navy U-boat during the First World War and sunk just 11 nautical miles from Ireland.[4]

He then described to me his last moment. It is May 7th 1915; mid-afternoon, so looking forward to seeing his family. He tells me he's a stoker and he maintains the steamship's furnace.

His final memories are of the ship filled with water and the anguish he felt at not being able to see his family again.

---

[4] https://en.wikipedia.org/wiki/The_Sinking_of_the_Lusitania

At that moment I separated Jonathan from his great-great-grandfather and told him what to say. These words were:

'I will honour your memories, but I can't and won't hang onto your misery any longer; all the agony, suffering, and unhappy feelings you had in life are not mine. It's unfair that I should shoulder the burden of your feelings of shame and remorse, and your inability to overcome the feeling of never wanting to leave home.

They are not mine, they are yours, and I must give them back to you.'

At that moment, the dark energy left Jonathan and entered his great-great-grandfather, which also released his traumas, sadness, and fears, as it's something he doesn't deserve to have. That moment a beautiful golden light fell down from the universe and surrounded them both with love and light.

He looked into his great-great-grandfather's eyes and saw love, relief and inner peace. His great-great-grandfather entered a doorway of light, looked back and smiled as he stepped through into the light.

You see they were both trapped in a doorway of time and they could not move on. You just can't imagine what his great-great-grandfather must have been going through.

I hope you the reader can now see the connection between that life and this life and the need for Jonathan to get home. And that he was reliving someone else's life.

The Loveday Method is a sophisticated technique for travelling through one's own consciousness in order to access inactive memories that are stored within one's Genes and are to blame for generational trauma. This can be accomplished by travelling back in time through the use of the Loveday Method.

This procedure is intended to provide therapy for memories that have been present in the family for a considerable period of time, and it is also intended to unearth the mysteries that are concealed within both our genes and our consciousness.

You can now see how effective The Loveday Method is...

Is it possible that you are reliving someone else's life and the feelings you are holding onto were there before you were born.

I cannot take credit for these questions. The original book was written by an extraordinary man with a vision.

"It Didn't Start With You", by Mark Wolynn.[5]

I need you to answer these questions:
These feelings of despair, anxiousness, sadness, and resentment that you currently hold, is it possible that a member of your family's past is the source of the unhappiness you're currently experiencing?

The final question: did it originate with you?

So now it's time to write your story and remember, you are not alone...

---

[5] Wolynn, M., 2017. It Didn't Start with You. Penguin Publishing Group, p.125.

Paul's Journey

"My name is Paul, and I am a big fan of positive thinking, hard work and hypnotherapy.

"I have a successful career in commercial law, my personal health, family, private relationship, and finances are all in good shape, I have everything that I always aimed for and am satisfied in life.

"I was fortunate to have enjoyed a perfect loving childhood, received an excellent education and I am highly qualified in my chosen profession. I enjoy my work and am very good at it, I love my family and my partner, I am quite comfortable in every respect, and I have no real personal problems.

"So why would I need to visit a hypnotherapist?

"Well, life has not always been like this, and whilst I am grateful to be in a good personal place now, I had to really dig deep to fight my way out of some difficult situations in the past.

"I can appreciate that some people are certainly not happy, and of course, all is not always well in the wider world.

"When the seasons approach the winter, around November, I usually notice that I start to feel strangely down and worried for no reason and talking to friends about it (not always a good idea) I wonder if I am suffering from some sort of weather affective disorder or weird malaise or apathy.

"It happened again this year and I just could not put my finger on what the problem was, or if one even existed. I just could not shake the feeling and having used a hypnotherapist ten years ago (to help with the management of grief) I knew that going deep into my subconscious would solve it.

"My first experience of hypnosis was an early Paul McKenna stage show many years ago, and at first having been highly sceptical, I came away from that show completely convinced of the power of hypnosis. I was fascinated at how it could no doubt be used for good and read a few of his books.

"I was browsing for a local hypnotherapist, found Geoff Loveday online, watched a few of his testimonials and read his book based on the theory that we are all a product of our ancestors.

"I have seen regression therapy on television and do enjoy the experience of deep trance and find it almost like relaxed assisted meditating. It is of course quite self-indulgent, but I thought why not?

"The answers to my thought problems came to the surface in quite an unexpected way.

"We were discussing the famous Dr Emoto 'rice' experiment and the psychological effects of 'self-talk' and the power of positive and negative thinking (I noticed a copy of the original 1956 Dr Norman Vincent Peale book in Geoff's office), and he was taking notes about my life history.

"My personal philosophy is that mental well-being in life is influenced by three circumstances. The past, the present and the future, but I had not ever considered the theory that genetics and hereditary mental health may *be related to the experiences and feelings of ancestors and can be passed down through the bloodline.*

"My parents are wonderful, strong-minded, loving people, and my grandparents were the same, and in fact proud members of the Queen's 'greatest generation'.

"In the first session, Geoff and I went into my personal past, and we found a couple of negative 'anger' issues which I had 'buried' since the worldwide credit crunch and financial crisis of 2008 had destroyed a previous business.

"These were dealt with in a positive way and the following years were celebrated (as they should be) for 'reinventing' myself and emigrating to start again in a much better location. The mentality of forgiving the past and celebrating victories however small is so important.

"I also discovered a family 'conference' where all four grandparents plus my parents and sister were sitting around a picnic table next to a beautiful lake which we used to visit in childhood.

"It was a lovely experience to all be together again and although nothing specific was discussed it was good to know that they are all fine and the feeling of them watching over us is the same as it always was.

"In the second session, I explained that I had found a way of dealing with some present uncertainty that had been unsettling and unbalancing me. These included a client renewing a contract plus a positive decision to accurately update my financial records and perhaps most importantly to stop listening to a negative and dysfunctional narrative which must have been affecting my own attitude.

"It was good to feel a positive affirmation within myself for finding the solutions and to hear the encouragement from Geoff for 'seeing the wood for the trees.' I remarked that it is almost like what I imagine a visit to a psychiatrist must be like (we have all seen it on American TV shows) and it was certainly good to 'get it off my chest' by explaining to an unconnected and impartial third party how I am tackling the present as well as the past (without rambling on about it to my family and friends).

"We then went into the deep trance state to do a bit of exploring by using the imagery that Geoff utilises with his clients of a staircase and a door into the subconscious mind and the wider universe.

"The answers I am looking for are an explanation and reasons for the surprisingly negative emotions and feelings I had in November and December about the immediate future. These were for the first time rattling my previously unshakeable confidence and affecting my ability to be 'bothered' about much at all, to the extent that I felt strangely 'lazy' and reluctant to work hard which is not like me.

"The regression was quite bizarre but felt safe and relaxed and I saw one of my grandfathers in what I can only describe as my 'mind's eye' … it was a bit like when Jim Carrey meets Morgan Freeman in 'Bruce Almighty' but without really speaking to each other, more of a 'feeling.'

"I then moved on to a sort of 'rainbow' coloured imagery which was almost like dreaming at Geoff's suggestions with childhood thoughts of 'Aladdin's

lamp' and seeking the pot of gold at the end of the rainbow.

"I found a paper message in the pot which said - 'you will be fine, don't worry about anything.'

"I think the message was one of reality because of course the lamp analogy and pot of gold idiom represent wishes and the pursuit of an ultimate financial goal which is difficult or impossible to achieve. I said in the opening paragraph that I have everything I aimed for, and that is true because in my younger days, the several goals I set for myself have been achieved, lost, and achieved again after a lifestyle of fighting back over a long period of time and I am very grateful for the ability to do that.

"I think the uncertainty came from the fact that I did not have that new contract at the time and was not certain that my efforts were being appreciated. I no longer have to fight but now the challenge is maybe setting myself new goals tempered by the amount of time left in life to achieve them. I was recently discussing this with an old friend talking about the relief of things we have achieved over the years and about future *investments and the global market which of course is far from certain.*

"*The other message I 'felt' rather than read was the fact that it was actually more difficult for past generations, and it was interesting that nothing was directly said to me by my grandparents when they were alive of any anxiety or fear during the tough times of the great depression of the 1930s when mass unemployment took hold or the second world war blitz of the 1940s when bombs were dropped on cities but there must have been times uncertainty existed within the minds of everyone.*

"*At the moment, after a relatively calm period of growth and prosperity up to 2020, the country has just gotten over the weird COVID pandemic, which was not good news at all, and we have the cost-of-living crisis and the war in Ukraine with German tanks rolling across the Russian border.*

"*The worldwide news right now all seems to be bad news, but the message is to have courage and not worry about issues which cannot be influenced by the individual but concentrate on happiness.*

"It felt good to know what the underlying issues are and to know that it is not just me concerned about current affairs, but even better to know that the answer and advice from past generations are again to go forward with courage and positive thinking and to know everything will be alright.

"Following the session yesterday I feel a new reassurance of calm optimism for the future and a strong sense of gratitude for the past and present – the negativity has already gone. The hypnotherapy works and I almost feel as if I have found a new and understanding good friend in Geoff and am really looking forward to completing the course and exploring what else we can do.

"He even threw in the bonus of helping me deal with my illogical fear of the dentist, and although I do not smoke cigarettes or drink to excess and am not scared of spiders or flying in aircraft, maybe a bit of subconscious encouragement and mental reinforcement to keep going with the enthusiasm for my fitness and diet goals for the purposes of feeling super healthy and enjoyment of work

in a fantastic busy industry for the purposes of future investment would be good?

"*I have read the accounts of some sports psychologists and was impressed by the discussions of the visualisation of winning and optimum performance by self-hypnosis by top athletes. The popularity of hypnotherapy also seems to be growing amongst certain successful business people.*

"*Mind over matter they used to call it ... positivity, optimism, love, fun, laughter, gratitude and hope are the ways forward and upwards to ultimate happiness .... Negativity, fear, complaints, pessimism, ignorance or hate, will send anyone down in the opposite direction .... Hypnotherapy has helped me to see that an attitude of gratitude and positive thinking or the opposite is a personal choice and will not just affect a container of rice one way or the other ... but the experience of the human brain.*

"*Hypnosis and self-hypnosis for me are almost spiritual experiences to be enjoyed and I would recommend Geoff Loveday to anyone .... In his hypnosis chair in a deep trance, it feels like being 'half-asleep'* and relaxed but with your capacity for imagination being 'switched on' and with the right guidance from such an expert in this field I firmly believe it is a powerful tool for well-being.

"I just re-read the section on Geoff's website about 'hypnoanalysis' and realised this is what we are actually working on ... for me there is a subtle difference between this and 'hypnotherapy' and this is the reason I decided to take the course ... to find the root cause of the problem and eradicate it.

"I will cooperate with the expert and enthusiastically continue with the sessions without drawing any further personal conclusions until we have completed the course – looking forward to it!!"

"Yours sincerely,
Paul Jones
February 2023"

Hypnotic Regression Analysis Session 3 – 04.03.23

"My mantra - my name is Paul, and I am a big fan of positive thinking, hard work, and hypnotherapy.

"My third session with Geoff took place at the usual early time on a Saturday morning, well before most people are awake or any traffic is on the road which always provides a nice sense of calm.

"Geoff asked me how I am feeling and mentioned that I could probably become a hypnotist myself because of my clear manner of speech. I took that as a big compliment, as it is something that I would really enjoy.

"The plan today was to regress back through time to see what we could find, and I mentioned to Geoff that I sometimes when waking up realise that I am thinking in an uncontrolled way or in a semi dream state when a low-level feeling of irrational fear over nothing can be present.

"We went through a routine in deep trance wherein Geoff guided me through how to 'minimise' and then 'cast out' or remove any such pointless negative thoughts and feelings and replace them in the subconscious mind with a beneficial sense of well-being in the present and optimism for the future.

"I was thinking on the way to the session how my life is very calm and relaxed nowadays, there is no drama, no risk, no stress, no fear, no fighting, and no major worries about anything in particular.

"This is in fact not a way of living that I was used to, because as I mentioned in my previous article, I have had to deal with some quite unpleasant past

"I am proud of my mental and physical discipline and am so very grateful if a higher power has assisted me in overcoming and dealing with those unexpected past difficulties and situations.

"I always wondered where I got the almost spiritual strength and fortitude to handle those situations that no one would wish on their worst enemy. I am not super religious, but I always thought there must be something guiding me. On the other hand, the human mind is a mystery.

"So, we went into a deeper regressive trance state to explore the Geoff's approach using The Loveday Method and I found myself in the imaginary Library opening a book on a page where there may be some indication of what traits might be in my family genes which may well have shaped my personality.

"I imagined myself in a battle trench in Belgium. It may have been on the Somme or Ypres in 1914 or 1916, amongst my great uncle and his brothers who were soldiers in the First World War. The fear was there but so was the courage and bravery and camaraderie.

"The early episodes of 'Peaky Blinders show the effects that war had on the mentality of the young men who had no choice but to fight or be killed and then came home and dealt with everyday working life in those days, a hard life.

"He was a bricklayer, fought right through to 1918 and became the nicest old gentleman ever.

"The second chapter was written in about 1925 and I was on a steam train handcuffed to a prisoner taking him to jail in Liverpool and I realised that I was my grandfather telling me the story of when he was a young policeman armed with a truncheon to make sure that they did not escape.

"The third chapter took place in 1940 when my other grandfather was responsible for building concrete anti-aircraft gun emplacements along the banks of the Mersey where I now live. Two of the three converted Victorian warehouse blocks were destroyed during the blitz by German bombers.

"The conclusions I drew from this book that I took with me from the 'dream state' were written on the last page by three very kind and very hard men, tough ancestors from my personal bloodline.

"They endured hardships and fearful situations beyond what we experience in our comfortable life today, many of them physically fought for our freedom using nothing but raw courage.

"Have courage and keep fighting if you have to – otherwise be grateful and enjoy this easy life."

"I considered myself told – and I have nothing but respect for the advice."

"Yours sincerely,
Paul Jones

March 2023"

Hypnotic Regression Analysis Session 4 – 11.03.23

"My mantra - my name is Paul, and I am a big fan of positive thinking, hard work, and hypnotherapy.

"My fourth session with Geoff took place at an even earlier time on a Saturday morning, crisp and cold after the late snow but with a hint of spring in the air.

"Geoff asked me how I am feeling, and I said that I am fine other than still occasionally thinking in an uncontrolled way in a semi-dream state when I am just waking up. The low-level feeling of irrational worry over nothing is sometimes still there so we decided to peel back the layers to investigate it.

"Further discussion revealed that it seems to be a fear of the future loss of loved ones which is of course irrational because it happens to everyone eventually. Human beings do not last forever in this world, but it may be that they go to a better one which should give us all comfort. Perhaps this is a historic existential question that all religions have had their own answer to since ancient Egypt and before.

"We are probably not going to solve the biggest mystery of life today, but it was a great conversation.

"So, we went into a deep regressive trance state, and I found myself looking at a map on a wooden sailing ship with a group of Naval Officers probably around 1850. If you have seen 'Master and Commander' starring Russell Crowe, you will get the idea.

"We are on our way to the United States to collect a grain shipment, and unfortunately have just lost one of the crew overboard and are feeling responsible and sad as the young lad had been drinking and apparently slipped and fell into the sea.

"There was a lot more discussion and detail in the session including an examination of that sense of corporate or legal responsibility as opposed to being personally responsible for someone else's misadventure. Geoff encouraged me to let go of any guilt for the death of the sailor and I felt better.

"The strangest thing after waking up from the trance was that I realised it had a direct similarity to something that happened to me in 2019. I work in the offshore construction industry as a manager and was based on an island in the Bahamas where an old cruise ship was docked and used as an accommodation vessel. The officer in charge of catering was also from Liverpool and there had been some controversy over the health and safety aspects of feeding kitchen food scraps to the sharks.

"The construction crews of 200 young lads, mostly locals or from South America were not allowed to drink alcohol which was banned from the ship and the island. The company management including myself had overall responsibility for ensuring the welfare and safety of the workforce on site.

"One morning there was a commotion in the office when it was reported that a worker was missing. Everyone was searching for him, and the police and coastguard were called. The searches went on for days and we were looking at the maps of the 'sweep' areas. The police interviewed the management and the lads, and it transpired that he had been drinking with his

mates at dusk and was chest deep in the water near the ship playing with a football when they left him alone.

"He had completely disappeared and the police concluded a bull shark had probably taken him. I have always had a fear of sharks since watching 'Jaws' many years ago (but am not scared of much else). Apparently, dusk is when they hunt and the most dangerous time to go in the sea especially up to chest height and especially if the water is full of food scraps when I see that they will eat anything.

"It was so very sad to witness the despair of his mother and sister who were flown from Argentina to visit his cabin on the island, and it upset us all in the Management team for a long time afterwards.

"It was so useful to have identified this deep-seated memory of guilt and Geoff and I went through an exercise to get rid of it and defined that there is not and was not much I could possibly have done to prevent that tragedy or any other human death for that matter and it was certainly not my fault.

"The positive mind-set that I took away from the session was an acceptance that we are all here on a journey and the best way to enjoy life is to focus on the good stuff. Gratitude for good health, love, and a beautiful calm, peaceful existence with no excessive stress, no fighting, and no fear.

"The main point to remember is that corporate responsibility is not personal. Guilt is something that needs to be removed from the mind, especially if not deserved, and forgiveness is wonderful.

"The left hand and the right hand in Geoff's hypnotic exercises are representatives of the positive and negative experiences in life and the importance is a realisation that there will be better and worse times which are beyond our control but are all part of the journey and part of life's rich tapestry.

"I could honestly have stayed chatting about life philosophy all day, but he had another Client straight after me. Perhaps I will invite him out for a pint or two when we have finished all the sessions."

"Yours sincerely,

Paul Jones
March 2023"

Hypnotic Regression Analysis Session 5 – 18.03.23

"My mantra - my name is Paul, and I am a big fan of positive thinking, hard work, and hypnotherapy.

"My fifth and penultimate session with Geoff made me think that I am going to miss the comfort and enjoyment of the Saturday morning 'cathartic' expressions of deep thought, but I feel the issues that were irritating me at the start of the winter are now largely resolved thanks to the outlet provided.

"I can still occasionally think in an uncontrolled way in a semi dream state when I am just waking up, so we decided to reinforce the previous exercise of 'neural pathway' subconscious control by removing the negativity, which clears up once I am awake and my conscious mind takes over.

"It was almost like 'having a word' with yourself to stop the mind wandering into negative thinking.

"The regression therapy part of the session this week revolved around a key to a door and the writing of a conclusion with an ink quill pen. Geoff mentioned his book and told me a fascinating story of self-belief in healing bodily illness which he is going to publish almost as a form of autobiography.

"Like me, he is a deep thinker and a firm believer in the power of the mind and positive self-talk. I was thinking on my way there how fortunate and grateful I am to be in such a relaxed position in life, my health, wealth, and relationships are all in good order and I am happy with all the fundamentals.

"The work remaining is to remove any 'silly' worries about losing people or losing anything else in the future because it is pointless, and the aim is to live life in the moment and enjoy our time on earth.

"The key and the quill pen represent unlocking what it is that I am really seeking and writing it down.

"The regression this week focussed on feeling of worry perhaps unintentionally passed down from a previous generation, and we again worked on 'casting it out.' At the end of the session, I felt calm.

"The final 'aspiration' was written down on the last page of the book which was unlocked by the key to the ultimate goal of what I am looking for in life – it was written down in ink in one phrase:

"Peace of Mind"

"After the session I was enjoying a 'zen' moment at home reflecting on a peaceful and quiet week of working from home when a friend called me.

"I sometimes don't take his calls because I know he is a proper 'conspiracy theorist' with strong and almost wacky 'cataclysmic' political opinions from the internet on everything from the Russians to the global Banking system. I cannot help thinking he will end up as one of those guys you see in town preaching through a microphone wearing a sandwich board with 'the end is nigh' printed on either side.

"On the other hand, we do have a long history and he has also survived some tough times in the past, but I do not take his ranting too seriously and treat it as 'catastrophizing' to be ignored. His attitude is the opposite of mine and I deliberately choose not to entertain any 'gallows humour' nowadays.

"Fortunately, my girlfriend has a similar light-hearted sense of humour as myself and we both prefer to laugh at daft stuff and sometimes end up in fits of giggles which is fantastic and so enjoyable.

"There is a time for taking things seriously, for me that is during working hours in my professional consultancy career in international energy business management, of which I am very proud.

"So in summary today my thoughts and my mood remains balanced, neutral and peaceful.

"I am looking forward to reading Geoff's next book and I will take him up on his suggestion that I may well make a reasonable hypnotist myself. Without breaking any 'patient confidentiality' he mentioned another interesting current Client, a pretty young woman who recently came to him with an issue of 'hating herself' when she looks in the mirror', which makes no sense.

"Very different Client from me but it would be fascinating to read about it and how hypnotherapy can help her."

"Yours sincerely,
Paul Jones
March 2023"

What Paul did not mention, before the second session he talked about the uncertainty about the future with all the things that are happening in the world today.

We took Paul to visit his grandfather in the 1930s 1940s he felt the fear of uncertainty of life and the future Paul felt the feelings of what his grandfather was going through.

Then we gave back the negative energy that Paul felt back to his grandfather and we released it from his grandfather.

I think you can understand how that life relates to this one today. And that he was experiencing events *from the life of another person. As well as continuing to be afraid.*

Do you still have some of their past fears?

Are you experiencing the same feelings as your ancestors?

Again on reading Paul's stories, you will see that he was in charge of other people's lives throughout each of his journeys.

Paul's existence has been greatly impacted by his responsibility to others; even today, he worries about his parents.

With the sense of loss and obligation we have for the people we love, this invisible impact influences not only Paul but people all over the world.

What Paul didn't mention during his fifth session was that he embarked on a journey to locate a missing key. He travelled back in time as his 10-year-old self to visit his grandfather, where he experienced the pain, emotions, and sorrow his grandfather endured. As a child, Paul had clung to the fear, anxiety, and uncertainty of life. However, during this session, he was able to release not only his own emotional pain but also those of his grandfather.

Put down on paper your thoughts and feelings about Paul and see if you arrive at the same conclusion I have, namely that his worries existed long before he was born and that our past can have a significant impact on our lives today.

So, tell me, do you have any fears?

So now it's time to write your story and remember you are not alone...

Jan's Story

This is just the beginning...

"Hi Geoff,

"This was the most amazing experience I've ever had. I was very doubtful at first as I've tried so many other things to stop my anxiety but nothing worked.

"During the first session, he made me see myself in my mum's womb, my first birthday, and another happy memory. Memories of me feeling loved and happy.

"Then he asked me to picture a door and me walking into the door, he asked me to describe the door, it was black and hardwood.

"He made me think of a memory that has made me feel anxious. My heart started racing, I was crying, and I got butterflies in my stomach. The fear was so real.

"He then wanted me to picture a lake, with my nan (who has passed), I started getting happy tears which felt amazing. He told me to imagine my Nan saying 'you

are strong, you don't need to hold on to this fear, I am watching you, I am taking this fear away from you'.

"He then wanted me to imagine her hugging me goodbye and letting her walk into the light. I was so shocked at how an unbelievable experience this was. Thank you Geoff for my first session, I can't wait to complete the course with you."

While reading Jan's story, you get the impression that she hoped I could transport her through time on a magical adventure to see her grandmother, who had passed away years before and help her overcome her fears.

On the other hand, it was only natural, she doubted that it could actually happen.

I have a question for you, the reader: do you believe it is possible for me to transport you back in time to visit a loved one who has passed away?

Did you say no? But just suppose I can? What exactly do you have to lose by trying?

In what ways could it help you?

So now it's time to write your story and remember you are not alone...

Sarah's Story

Sarah came to see me suffering from depression anxiety and low self-esteem. She had an eight year battle with body dysmorphia. Her one wish was to be happy.

Body dysmorphia is a mental health condition in which a person becomes preoccupied with perceived flaws or defects in their physical appearance, often to the point of obsessiveness.

People with body dysmorphia may spend hours each day trying to hide or fix their perceived flaws, or they may avoid social situations altogether.

Body dysmorphia can affect people of any age, gender, or ethnicity, and it can lead to significant distress and impairment in daily functioning. It is often accompanied by other mental health conditions such as anxiety and depression.

Treatment for body dysmorphia typically involves therapy, medication, or a combination of both. Cognitive-behavioural therapy (CBT) has been found to be particularly effective in helping individuals with body dysmorphia to change their negative thoughts and behaviours. Medications such as selective serotonin reuptake inhibitors (SSRIs) may also be prescribed to help alleviate symptoms.

A meeting with my Great Grandmother

"My first experience of hypnotherapy with Geoff was better and more successful than I ever could have imagined. Our aim across 6 sessions is to build my self-confidence regarding my appearance by conquering my eight-year long battle with body dysmorphia.

"The session started with me shutting my eyes and laying down in bed while via a zoom call Geoff guided me through the hypnosis, prompting me to recall the original situation my self-esteem anxiety had originated from, back from when I was ten years old where my mother put makeup on me to enhance my physical appearance.

"From then on I learnt that I was only attractive to others with makeup on, thus sparking my deeply unhealthy self-reliance on makeup, because I didn't like how my natural face looked.

"Geoff also asked me to recall any moments outside of this initial encounter with my mother where my self-dependence on makeup was reinforced, and helped me remember times where my mother commented that I looked ill and pale, reinforcing the need I felt to put makeup on to enhance my complexion. Geoff helped me realise that my self-esteem anxiety had come from my mother's own insecurities, that had been passed onto her from her mother, and so on.

"Geoff then asked me to envision myself in my safe place to take me to a calm, emotionally secure setting. I did so, and following this, he asked me to imagine my mother in front of me bound up with duct tape so she couldn't speak back, and knowing she could only listen to what I had to say, what would I tell her.

"This offered me a gateway to explore my true, deep feelings that had been pent up over the past eight years, where I got everything off my chest – this was quite an emotional experience for me as it allowed me to say things I had never said out loud before and surprised myself with some of my unconscious thoughts that had been allowed to finally surface.

"After expressing myself, Geoff asked me to envision him touching my forehead, and at his touch all the negative energy I had been harbouring over the years slowly came out of my body. He asked me what colour it was and I responded with dark purple.

"In that moment I truly felt dark purple energy leaving my body, and Geoff helped me see it leave my mother's body as well. Once it had all escaped, I was told to envision a bright white light seeping down from above and entering both of our bodies, purifying us of all the negative energy that our bodies had been burdened with all these years.

"When I was coming to the end of my hypnosis, Geoff asked me to open my eyes to bring me back to reality and I remember feeling incredibly light in my body. He asked how I felt and in that moment I felt wonderful, like a huge sack of weights had fallen right off my back.

"Finally, Geoff simply asked me to envision a flight of stairs. I did so, and he asked me if they were going up or down, to which I replied 'up.' He then told me to slowly ascend the stairs, at my own pace, until I reached a door at the top.

"I turned the doorknob and stepped outside, and Geoff asked me where I was. I was in a meadow full of flowers and sunshine, and my mother and father were there with me. Geoff guided me through another hypnosis, where I walked down a path with my parents through the beautiful meadow until a figure walked forward.

"Geoff asked me who this figure was, and it didn't necessarily have to be someone I had met before. I replied without hesitation that it was my great-grandmother, and although I didn't really know what she looked like given I had never met her, I had utmost confidence it was her.

"Geoff informed me that this was where my body dysmorphia had originated from, as my unconscious mind had led me here, and asked me to take her hand. We walked away from my parents until we were alone, and once again I watched as the dark purple cloud from earlier escaped her body, and she was cleansed like me and my mother had been earlier with bright light.

"At this moment in my hypnosis, a rainbow emerged over my head, as if all the negative energy had been fully eradicated and replaced with positivity and self-love.

"I awoke again from my hypnosis feeling so light in my body it could have been empty. I even struggled sitting upright in bed because I felt like my body had truly been purified of everything that had been existing in it for years. I felt so appreciative of Geoff's compassion and commitment to helping me, as he communicated his empathy for me all the way through the session, enabling me to feel secure and supported."

A Journey into Space

"My second experience of hypnotherapy with Geoff was mainly focused on reinforcing the same positivity of the first session and revisiting the same themes. Once I closed my eyes again Geoff guided me through the hypnosis, prompting me to imagine my arms represented light, warmth and success, and they would rise the more I started to let those things into my body.

"When I opened my eyes my arms were high in the air – then Geoff asked me to imagine letting go of any negative, insecure feelings but only 50% of these, and upon opening my eyes I saw my arms were still raised but had dropped to a midway point representing the 50% loss of negative emotions. We did this again at 25% until we reached 0% and my arms were gently rested across my lap.

"Geoff prompted me to imagine I was travelling through time in a ball of light, entering different universes, I saw a lady 1700s felt her pain which I released. Then I found myself on a desert sandy island in the middle of the sea.

"He guided me to follow a path on the island and once I did a rainbow of colours enveloped me, each one representing something different that I had to welcome into my heart, for instance self-love and confidence.

"He then asked me to find the end of the rainbow, where there were words written on a plaque, and asked me what words were waiting for me. I answered, "You have found self-love."

"Then I went into the rainbow, feeling its positivity and warmth once more, cleansing me further of any negative emotion, and enabling me to feel much lighter than I had before the session. I felt myself smile a lot throughout the hypnosis as Geoff's empathy and comedy helped me feel appreciated as a human being, and beautiful. I was ready to take on the day and felt like it was a wonderful way to start the morning."

You will be able to see a significant improvement after just one session. You will observe that the insecurities she felt were not only inherited from her mother but also from her great-grandmother.

After you've finished reading Sarah's story, take a moment to reflect on your own life and determine whether or not there is a connection between your own family background and an issue that you're currently experiencing.

So now it's time to write your story and remember you are not alone...

Leah's Story

Leah, who is currently 31 years old, recently visited me on Tuesday, May 30th, 2023. Despite the passage of time, the loss of her mother when she was just 10 years old continues to have a profound impact on Leah's life. This lingering impact has resulted in feelings of depression, anxiety, unhappiness, and a sense of being lost. Leah is also a mother herself, with two beautiful daughters.

I asked her, if she had one wish what would it be?

Her answer was to see her mum again. Please take the time to read her story...

The moment of magic - *The story of the dream that became reality...*

"From the moment I closed my eyes to lie back and relax the door at the top of the stairs opened. Although my eyes were closed, a new memory opened that I can now treasure forever. Seeing an angel in what I can only describe as a white gown waiting in the distance to greet me and her 2 grandchildren she's never met.

"Although I believed she'd never met the children, in this moment it was as though she'd always been around; which now I believe she is. My children ran and hugged her and for what felt like minutes, we hugged and hugged some more and she told me she loved me and things will be okay.

"Leah." To hear my name from the woman who brought me into this world, the woman who I'd never believed I would hear her voice around me again, the only thing that mattered here was time and to take in these precious moments for as long as I could.

I then received a gift from my angel, which was a key, which I believe was the key to lock away all the pain I'd suffered, and all the hurt and negativity in my life, and leave it all behind the door I'd walked through.

Never will I get this moment again, but never will I need this moment to make me realise my mum is here, my mum is me, and my mum is everything positive *around me. And I'll be forever grateful to of experienced such a magical gift..."*

I invite you, as the reader, to share your thoughts on Leah's experiences following the loss of her mother and the root causes of her suffering in life.

Additionally, please reflect upon whether there exists a connection between your upbringing and the challenges you faced during your youth, and how those experiences continue to influence your present life.

Now, it is your turn to write your story, bearing in mind that you are not alone in this journey...

PART FOUR

Your Story

All About You

Now it's your turn.

The reason I thought it was crucial for you to become involved with the book is not just because of the individuals I've helped in the past. The book was created specifically in order to help you, the reader.

Now, I want you to take some time out of your day and compose a piece of writing in which you primarily focus on who you are.

Put your feelings down on paper.

Let the sorrow isolation anxiety sadness and worry move back and focus on getting to know yourself, and discover your true identity.

So now it's time to write your story and remember you are not alone...

Your story...

Now when you have written in detail about yourself, I want you to find a quiet place where you can sit down and close your eyes for 10 minutes and be in the moment.

You will do this for 30 days

Visualisation and Meditation.

When the imagination and the conscious mind are in conflict, imagination always wins.

During this time of peace and quiet, your attention will be drawn to the people whom you believe have hurt you; you will picture these individuals in great detail in your thoughts.

You will not be able to avoid them, and you will have no choice but to confront your anxieties, sadness, and unhappiness regardless of what you are clinging to.

- *You will not run away from life.*
- *You will not run away from yourself.*
- *You will face your fears head-on.*
- *You are not weak, you are strong.*

Once you face these fears in the form of the individuals they have become, you will look them in the eyes and repeat these words:

'I won't hold the pain and misery you have caused me. The sorrow, misery, and dread I am experiencing

are not my feelings; instead, they are yours. The things you feel the insecurities that you have is yours not mine. I have to give these feelings back to you as you release this dark energy not only see it but also feel it, feel it leave you and enter them and as it enters them it releases their trauma, their sadness and fear, something they don't deserve to have.'

You will experience a sense of inner calm at that precise time when a beautiful golden light falls from the universe, surrounds you with love, and drives out the darkness.

At this moment really feel this beautiful golden light. When you feel that sense of inner calm nod your head. You will then look into their eyes. As you do, what are they trying to tell you? When you look into their eyes, what do you feel?

I then want you to forgive them.

Repeat these words out loud.

'I forgive you because forgiving you sets me free. I forgive you because now I can let go. I forgive you because now you have no control over my life.'

You will do this to each individual you feel has caused you pain. Once you have released everything, you will invite the "you" as a little child, you will put your arms around him or her and tell them they are not to blame; it is not their fault

Repeat out loud:

'We will not live this way anymore. We will not hold onto the pain of others. We have to release this dark energy back to whoever and wherever it came from, as you do see the darkness leave you not only see it but also feel it.'

It is so important to feel the energy. As you see this happen a beautiful golden light covers you both and replaces the darkness that has just left you with love and light.

At that moment the little child will melt inside you like the colours of the rainbow part of you that you have lost now is part of you.

It then recharges the seven stars inside you; the seven chakras, the life force within you. When you feel you are ready then you will open your eyes.

You will do this for 30 days, and I want you to notice subtle changes.

PART FIVE
Belief

Belief

Belief is a psychological state in which an individual holds a conviction or assumption to be true. Ultimately, belief is a powerful force that drives individuals and can shape their lives in meaningful ways.

Beliefs are an essential part of who we are, so it is important to take the time to reflect on what we believe and why. By doing this, we can better understand ourselves and others, leading to greater acceptance for all individuals no matter their beliefs.

By recognising the importance of belief, we can create a more compassionate and understanding world.

The power of belief should never be underestimated. It is an integral part of who we are and drives our behaviours and attitudes towards the world at large.

Beliefs shape how we engage with the people around us and what values we strive to uphold. It is important to understand our own beliefs and those of others to create a more accepting and understanding world. By recognising the power of belief, we can use it to promote growth and foster acceptance for all.

To talk to a loved one who has passed.

I understand how difficult it is to believe. I understand you want to think that it is possible, but you must first experience it to genuinely believe.

So I would like you to take a leap of faith.

A video has been made just for you to take you on a journey to experience something magical.

Watch the video here…
https://www.inheritedtherapy.com

PART SIX

The Journey

The Journey

Step by step, I can show you how it is possible. One of our dedicated practitioners will guide you on a journey you will never forget.

A programme of 6 sessions, these sessions will change your life.

Stage 1: The Pre-Talk

A thorough review of the client's history will occur during the pre-talk. It will be extremely obvious to you after listening that the feelings you have been holding onto existed before you were even created.

After the pre-talk, appointments will be set up if you think it's for you and you want our help; otherwise, there won't be a charge.

When working with children up to the age of 18, a parent must be present.

Stage 2: Depth of Trance.

Step 1: The Change.
Step 2: The Akashic library.

Step 3: A magical journey.

Step 4: Inner peace.

Step 5: The Crystal.

Step 6: A new beginning.

Step 7: A journey you will never forget.

The first step is to speak to one of our dedicated practitioners who have been trained by me in Inherited Therapy and The Loveday Method.

There you have it; the help you desperately need is here, to visit the people you have lost.

So let the journey begin.

For information visit these sites.
https://www.inheritedtherapy.com
https://www.liverpoolhypnosis.co.uk

Or contact me on:
geof@inheritedtherapy.com

❖

Look out for my next book, the Fourth in the series of Seven, Coming Out in October 2023.

How to Reprogram A Child's Mind Through the Power Of Storytelling.

The Loveday Method: Part 4

"The Magical Journey For Children"

A must-read for children with unwanted thoughts that will give your child hope.

A journey into the stories of the mind.

Bibliography

1. *https://en.wikipedia.org/wiki/Albert_Einstein*
2. *https://community.thriveglobal.com/einstein-letter-to-his-daughter-on-the-universal-force-of-love/*
3. *https://en.wikipedia.org/wiki/Third_eye*
4. *https://en.wikipedia.org/wiki/The_Sinking_of_the_Lusitania*
5. *Wolynn, M., 2017. It Didn't Start with You. Penguin Publishing Group, p.125.*

www.ingramcontent.com/pod-product-compliance
Lightning Source LLC
Chambersburg PA
CBHW030110100526
44591CB00009B/355